William R. (William Rathbone) Greg

Rocks Ahead

The Warnings of Cassandra

William R. (William Rathbone) Greg

Rocks Ahead
The Warnings of Cassandra

ISBN/EAN: 9783744667210

Printed in Europe, USA, Canada, Australia, Japan

Cover: Foto ©Thomas Meinert / pixelio.de

More available books at **www.hansebooks.com**

ROCKS AHEAD;

OR,

THE WARNINGS OF CASSANDRA.

BY

W. R. GREG.

SECOND EDITION,

WITH A REPLY TO OBJECTORS.

Mr Pitt—I have no fear for England: she will stand till the Day of Judgment.
Mr Burke—It is the day of no judgment that I dread.

LONDON:
TRÜBNER & CO., 57 & 59 LUDGATE HILL.
MDCCCLXXIV.

All rights reserved.

CONTENTS.

A

PREFACE

TO

THE SECOND EDITION,

———o———

REPLY TO CRITICS AND OBJECTORS.

I HAVE read the various comments and criticisms
which have appeared on "Rocks Ahead" with
much care and with a sincere desire to find that
I had omitted or under-estimated some considerations which might throw doubt on the conclusions
I put forward, or at least mitigate their gloomy
character. I have profited by some of the suggestions offered to modify, in the collected and
amplified form which the Papers in the *Contemporary Review* have now assumed, a few of
the expressions originally used, and to develop a
few points more fully and more clearly, as well
as to discuss one or two objections which appeared
to me more valid than the rest. But I cannot
say that I find any one of my conclusions to have
been materially shaken, nor any of my statements

or arguments successfully impugned. I should have been glad if it were otherwise; for the subject is far too grave for egotism, and the picture I drew of the probable future of my country too sad, both in colouring and outline, to be dwelt upon by any patriot without pain. But most of my critics have been contented either to represent my views as the morbid exaggerations of a writer notorious for the consistent lugubriousness of his temperament, and habitually a *laudator temporis acti, se puero, castigatorque minorum*—which may be very true, but is surely somewhat irrelevant;—or to assert in jaunty confidence that with a people so energetic and full of solid good sense as we are, "something is sure to turn up" to avert the prognosticated evil,— which is possible, of course, but which one would fancy could comfort those only who really believe that we *are* so exceptionally sound, sensible, cautious, and forecasting, or who are content to trust to the chapter of accidents to prevent active causes issuing in natural results.

Here and there, however, an antagonist has taken up a more distinct and hostile position, and has professed to show that my premises are inaccurate and incomplete, my arguments invalid, and my philosophy and economy essentially and flagrantly unsound as well as shallow. One writer in particular, in the September number of the *Contemporary Review*, has attempted so elaborate a refutation of all my positions as to call for a somewhat more detailed reply. Not that I propose to drag my readers through a prolonged controversy which would be an abuse of their patience, and unnecessary for my purpose ; much of Mr Arthur Arnold's paper consisting of such slight misrepresentation or misplacement of my views as was needed to bring them within the range of his guns—a very common but not a very profitable tactical proceeding. I will only comment on a few of the more essential points where we seem to be utterly at variance.

But, first, there are some expressions and more implications in Mr Arnold's attack of which I think I have just reason to complain. It is of course too much to expect that a critic should be acquainted with the antecedents and general views of the man against whom his criticisms are directed, but in the absence of that acquaintance he should surely abstain from language at once incriminating and curiously inappropriate. He not only in two or three passages uses expressions implying ignorance on my part of the working classes, and his own superior information, but he charges me with "looking at the working man *de haut en bas*," of "writing of them with superb patronage," considering them "stupid," and of speaking of them "in a manner most odiously pharisaical."

Now, I do not know what may have been the temporary opportunities of intimacy with the artisan class which Mr Arnold's experience may have given him, but I shall be surprised to learn that it can equal those of one who for twenty-five of the best years of his life was closely bound up with that class, not only as a large employer of labour and a large owner of cottage dwellings, but as an earnest and industrious, though perhaps not very efficient, labourer for their improvement and comfort; and who for another twenty-five years has made their interests his ceaseless study, and the main object of continuous political and literary efforts. Mr Arnold may have looked at them, visited them, inspected them, "superintended" them:—I may fairly claim to have lived among them, toiled for them, sympathised with them, spoken the truth to them as well as of them, served them, but never flattered them. I do not, indeed, like Lord Shaftesbury, profess to "reverence" them. I cannot, like Mr Arnold (p. 637) regard them as pure incarnations of political wisdom, who, in pursuit of their own interests, are sure to go just as far as they ought to do, and no further,—because I do not see that they have usually done this, or are doing it now;—but I respect them, value them, am hopeful about them, on account of their sterling and manly qualities, and their frequent shrewd sense when not misguided and demoralised by those who seek their suffrages or would gain the use of their strength. And what, I may ask, is there so " odiously pharisaical "—so redolent of " the sublime height of a morganatic alliance with the Gods" (whatever that may mean) in saying that the English working men, "properly trained, properly led, properly dealt with, would make out and out the best Proletariat in the world," and that they are (apart from their drinking propensities) " more intelligent, more fair, and more sober-minded than those of other lands?" Does Mr Arnold, who professes himself so disgusted with my phrase, mean that they need no training and no guidance,—and that while " inferior in his opinion in the points I mention to the working classes of most other countries," they are still —and now—fit to govern their own country, and to outvote all other classes? Several passages in his paper appear to indicate that he is

xii ROCKS AHEAD.

prepared to defend this advanced thesis, and
to maintain that the great body of the labouring
class may not only be safely intrusted with the
ruling power, but are more likely better qualified to exercise it honestly and sagaciously than
those above them in the social scale. If so the
difference in our views is no doubt considerable
and fundamental ; and we may leave the decision
to our readers. Mr Arnold deems it "the first,
indeed the whole, duty of a Statesman to learn
the will of the people, and to follow that"—the
people here meaning, as the context shows, the
majority, the masses. I should call such a man
a tool, a slave, a minister perhaps—certainly not
a Statesman. I need only point out that the
classes whom he thinks it desirable thus to endow
with paramount political influence in the State
are, in his view, and according to his wide
acquaintance with the Proletariat of Europe, "in
the matters of wisdom, self-respect, and self-
control, behind all other nations" (p. 633). Mr
Arnold says I call them "stupid :" I took pains
to say just the reverse.

In one point my assailant and I agree ; and
that point is so important that it might, I should
have hoped, have led Mr Arnold to regard me as
rather an ally than an antagonist. We are both

earnest advocates of the diffusion of property—
especially property in land—among the labouring
poor ;—only that he considers this as the great
object for which their political supremacy is to
be desired, while I look to it as the chief safe-
guard against the possible dangers growing out
of that political supremacy.   Here, too, however,
I note a certain inconsistency among his statements and his aspirations, arising apparently from
irrepressible democratic animosities.   He more
than once refers to Lord Derby's assertion that
" the produce of the English soil might be
doubled" as conclusive proof that " the interest
of the masses has been habitually disregarded by
the upper classes," and that this deficient productiveness is due to the non-ownership of land by
the peasant order, and would be cured by a change
in the proprietary body.   He can scarcely be
conversant with the careful investigations of M.
Léonce de Lavergne, who shows that of every
article of agricultural produce the average yield
in England, where the soil is held in few hands,
is *double* that in France, the land *par excellence*
of peasant proprietorship, wide subdivision, and
garden culture.   Probably, too, notwithstanding
" his personal acquaintance with the people of
every European State," he would be surprised to

b

find that the average annual produce of wheat in Belgium (which seems to be his land of promise) is at least 25 per cent. below that of England.* He mentions *five or even eight hundred millions* sterling as the amount of capital which must be applied to agriculture in our country in order to bring up its productiveness to a proper standard, and declares that capital will not be thus liberally lavished on the soil till " a vast diffusion of property in land shall have taken place." He overlooks the fact that the free application of capital, and above all of machinery, to agriculture takes place where large properties and not peasant properties prevail;—and that one of the great drawbacks upon small holdings is that capital is rarely forthcoming, and that machinery is scarcely applicable. In a word, my critic is so little careful either of his logic or his facts that, while

* The following comparative yield is given on the authority of two passages by different authors in the " Cobden Club Essays "—a work which Mr Arnold will, I apprehend, admit to be reliable. —I. p. 431, II. p. 166 :—

AVERAGE PRODUCTION OF WHEAT.

	Bushels per Acre.	Hectolitres per Hectare.
Great Britain, . . .	28	40
Holland, ...	...	23
Prussia, ...	17	19¾
Belgium, ...	21	19¼
Italy, ...	...	16
France, ...	14	14½

clamouring for the application of capital to land on a portentous scale, he is equally eager for a subdivision of the land among the class which is peculiarly short of capital; and then selects for animadversion the special set of landowners who have sunk more capital in their land than those of any other country, and *have got*—climate considered—*a larger produce out of their land;* and finally represents them as proving, by the scantiness of that produce, their habitual disregard of the interest of the consuming class ! And this is the critic who so " complains of Mr Greg's three papers, on account of their fallacious parade of care, with a show of calculation which is not borne out upon anything like critical examination."

It is much to be wished that so ardent an advocate as Mr Arnold of the diffusion of property in the soil among the peasant and artisan classes, would have addressed himself to the problem I propounded in a note (p. 45, or p. 878 in the *Review*,) in the first " Rock Ahead "—a problem of which I have as yet seen no attempt at solution. How—in a country like England, where every rich man is eager to buy land, and willing to give far more for it than it is economically worth — is the peasant proprietor to be *secured* in the possession of his holding? that is, to be restrained from selling it on the very advantageous terms which are certain to be offered him? Still more, how, when his small property is made still smaller by subdivision among his children, is each one of them to be withheld from parting with his field for five or ten times its value? This has always appeared to me the greatest practical difficulty which we, who desire the wider distribution of landed property among the masses, have to meet.

I will not follow Mr Arnold in his comments on my second "Rock Ahead." He simply "pooh-poohs" from the height of his superior knowledge or keener insight, all the dangers which I gave grounds for believing were real and visible, however distant. The idea of our cheap coal being worked out, he scouts, as in his judgment mere nonsense. Coal, he affirms, is not getting dearer or scantier, nor will it do so. "Coal is relatively as cheap now as it was in 1834, and there is no reason to suppose that it will not be relatively as cheap in 1900 as it is at present." This is random talk, calling for no reply. I need only say that his dictum will not be endorsed by men far better qualified than either he or I to form an opinion.

Again : he considers my notion that where machinery is largely involved, or is the real productive agency, a reduction of the hours of labour
means an *approximate* reduction in the produce
of that labour, to be mere moonshine ; and he
undertakes to contradict it on his own authority.
I spoke with *connaissance de cause ;* I gave fully
the grounds and reasons for my conclusion ; I
have nothing to add to them ; and I am no way
shaken in my estimate of their validity.   Mr Arnold treats my apprehension of the future probability and gradual approach of serious foreign
competition in several departments of our industry, with the usual airy disdain of the ordinary
British Philistine.   I did not speak without book ;
and (stated with the guarded moderation with
which I stated it) my position, I am satisfied, is
unassailable.   Mr Hugh Mason's opinion is, no
doubt, a weighty one ; but his confidence is not
shared by others equally qualified to judge.   And,
observe, I did not speak of the danger to our
trade and industry from foreign competition as a
thing [that now is, but as a thing that, if not
averted, must come from causes ahead, imminent
or in operation,*—and I should be grieved indeed

* It is only two or three weeks since a very impressive and well-
informed paper maintaining in detail those facts and menaces of

to regard the insane armaments of continental Europe (which Mr Mason very justly considers as one of our present most efficient safeguards against the danger in question) as permanent facts of modern history.

Mr Arnold attributes to me (as the *Spectator* had done before him) an ignorance or oversight of one of the clearest principles of political economy, which he specifies as the foundation of most of my blunders. " Mr Greg is really the victim of one of the most hoary and inveterate of economic fallacies." . . . . " He has incautiously fallen headlong into the fallacy, that the increase of our neighbours must be our undoing." . . . . " Mr Greg's fundamental error lies in confounding our relative position, which of course declines as other countries approach a higher level of industrial and mechanical industry, with our actual position as regards wealth and comfort in the future." I am supposed not to perceive that " it must be a benefit to us, as it is to individual tradesmen, to live among wealthy neighbours :" and my " error is so patent, so curious, and in so able a man so startling," that Mr Arnold is " almost inclined to apologise for setting forth such

which Mr A.'s omniscience makes so light, was read at the Social Science Meeting at Glasgow by Mr Matheson.

elementary facts in commercial science by way of refutation." The *Spectator* puts the matter still more strongly : " Mr Greg's error is really closely allied to that old Protectionist fancy, that one nation suffers by the development of the resources of other nations, instead of gaining by it. Nothing is more certain, we take it, than that it is for England's *advantage*, to put it plainly, *that she should lose her commercial supremacy*, if she loses it by no wasteful blunder of her own, but solely by the legitimate development of such of the resources of other nations, as were hitherto unknown or unused."

Now, much of this I have already answered in the second edition of my papers, to which I may refer Mr Arnold and his readers ; the rest whether consisting of confusion or truism, seems to me simply irrelevant.   I am not such a tyro in economic science as to be unaware that the increasing wealth of the world at large must be an indirect benefit to every country in the world ; nor am I so devoid of ordinary perception as not to recognise that it is far better for a trading country, as for an individual tradesman, to live among wealthy neighbours, *so long as those neighbours are customers*.   But what bearing have all these platitudes upon my position ?   I simply

pointed out that hitherto England's exceptional
advantages had given her an exceptional position,
and had made a very small nation into a very
great one; that, being in certain specified par-
ticulars so far ahead of other countries, she had
manufactured for them and supplied their wants,
and to this was owing her rapid and continued
progress in prosperity—a prosperity increasing
just as the wealth and wants of her neighbours
increased; that this rate of progress could not go
on, and would probably in time decline as those
neighbours began to supply their own wants, and
ceased to come to us for various articles as of
yore; and that, just in proportion as the cost of
production in this country augmented, would the
rival and superseding production of other countries be stimulated. Is there any one of these
propositions that Mr Arnold seriously fancies he
has overthrown, or even that he can contest?
" We cannot," he admits, " be spinners and
weavers for all the world." Very true; we
cannot continue to be so; that is just what I
allege; but the point is that *we have been
so and are beginning to cease to be so;* and that
as our customers fall off or go elsewhere we shall
have to curtail our production, or cease to extend
it; that such curtailment or non-extension implies

a check to our progress and our population; and
that such check, if not foreseen and provided for,
will involve much distress and suffering. Is any
one of these allegations impugnable? Mr Arnold
and the *Spectator* seem to find consolation in the
jaunty assumption that even if we cease to provide the textile fabrics and the coal and iron of
the world, there will always be something else
which the world will want and which we shall
be preferentially applied to provide. But the
very same causes which make our coal and iron
and woollens and calicos dearer than those of
other lands, will affect more or less all our productions. "But all your customers are getting
richer," argues Mr Arnold, " and can afford therefore to purchase more and to give higher prices."
*What is that to me if they cease to come to my
shop?* Will America, merely because she is
wealthy, buy her iron rails from England, while by
reason of excellent coal and ore in Pennsylvania
in proximity to the surface and to each other, she
can manufacture them *more* cheaply for herself?
Will Japan, or Russia, or Italy, or renovated Asia,
however rich they may grow, come to us for their
metals or their woven goods when the United
States, or Belgium, or Switzerland, can supply
them at a lower cost, and make a profit by doing

so ? I say that *if* our coal and iron fail us, *when* they fail us, and *in proportion as* they fail us, the productions we supply to other countries, and which we have prospered and grown affluent by supplying, will become more costly and more scarce, and that we shall be less and less resorted to for them ; and that thus a great source of our hitherto income will be cut off. Is Mr Arnold prepared to dispute the proposition ? " Oh," but he says, " that is all gloomy nonsense ; iron and coal won't fail us; and if our wares do get dearer, what will that matter so long as our customers grow richer, and are all able and willing to pay us more ! " This seems to be pretty much the state of the controversy between us, and I may leave it here. Only I cannot exactly comprehend the logical process of a mind which does not per- ceive that a nation which has grown rich by the possession and use of a vast treasure hidden in its soil, must grow poorer, positively as well as rela- tively, by the exhaustion of that treasure. Mr Arnold may have intended to argue—I believe the *Spectator* did—that *England must pay for her imports*, and that the countries with which she trades, rather than not deal with her, will take her iron and textile fabrics in payment, even though these are dearer than their own, or than those of other lands. Doubtless to some extent this may be the case ; but a far surer operation and consequence will be that as England loses her productive advantages, and thereby reduces her productiveness, *she will have to restrict her imports*—an idea which my critics do not seem to have taken in. Nations, like individuals, when they lose a large source of their wealth by the exhaustion of the balance at their bankers (whether that balance be gold in their coffers or iron or coal beneath the soil), must reduce their purchases, or become bankrupt. As to the dictum of the *Spectator* that " it will be for England's national *advantage* to lose her commercial supremacy"—if " economical" advantage be meant, as by the context I suppose it must be—I can only class it among the daring paradoxes with which that very clever but sensational journal delights to startle or tickle its readers. England's "commercial supremacy" signifies only her power of supplying an inordinate proportion of the wants of the world by underselling all competitors. How it can be for the advantage of her wealth to lose this power, needs, I think, a little explanation.

In conclusion, I would wish to remind my readers that I have been no prophet in the ordinary sense of that word. I have not predicted that the evils treated of *will* come upon us. I have merely pointed out certain agencies in operation, or visibly approaching, which must bring about those evils, unless counteracted in time by other agencies not yet efficient or in sight. I hope the mischiefs I signalised may be averted : I have endeavoured to show how they may be averted ; but I am sure that those who deny their imminence or their likelihood are not taking the wisest means to avert them.—Meanwhile my opponents, be their arguments good or bad, are sure to have the best of it before the public. The world, which turns with disgust from my grave forebodings, will hail their delusive comfortings with a shout of welcome or a sigh of relief. The prophets who cry " Peace, peace," when there is no peace, have a pleasant time of it—till war comes. No nation will prepare for the evil day, so long as there are seers in abundance who assure them *ex cathedrâ* that the evil day is very distant or very problematic, or (better still) that it exists only in the morbid imagination of a pessimist by temperament. They will be listened to and caressed, while I shall be laughed at ; and the nation, soothed by their opiates into fatal slumbers, will

turn on its pillow and address itself, as before, to
dreams of endless luxury and sunshine.

> " Cassandra's fate reversed is theirs ;—
> She, true, no faith could gain ;
> They every passing hour deceive,
> Yet are believed again."

On Lord Lyttleton's commentary I have no remarks to make, beyond thanking him for the
courtesy and kindly appreciative tone of his language towards myself—a tone so unhappily rare
among controversialists. I am too well aware
that the Christianity which I would fain see
taught, as the only form likely in the end to hold
its ground in this country, must appear to Lord
Lyttleton a creed shorn of all its more specifically
valuable and essential elements.

Mr Grant Duff has done me the honour to
make this volume the text of an address delivered
on the 30th of October, at the opening of the
Philosophical Institution of Edinburgh, and since
published in the *Fortnightly Review*. The commentary is for the most part a dissentient one;
that is, he deems my general views far too gloomy,
and thinks I have overlooked or greatly under-
estimated the re-cuperative powers of a nation still
healthy at the core ; but when we come to close

quarters I cannot perceive that he seriously questions any of my premises, or decisively demurs to
any of my conclusions.   On the contrary, most of
both he avowedly or implicitly admits.   The
address, therefore, interesting as it is, because of
the thoughtful and suggestive remarks scattered
through its pages, I can scarcely persuade myself
to look upon as even an attempted refutation of
my argument.   Mr Grant Duff and I seem to differ
scarcely more than thinkers of discrepant temperaments must differ, even when dealing with the same
facts, and holding the same general principles.   He
is an optimist, who thinks that all will go right, and
that because we have improved so greatly in the
past, we shall certainly go on improving in the
future.   I am—not a pessimist, I hope, but merely
an observer who wishes to look probable perils in
the face in time, believing that, however avert-
able, they will not be averted if they are resolutely
ignored or gilded over.   Perhaps the divergence
in our hopes and estimates may be due merely to
the circumstance, that he is a much younger man
than I am ; identically the same sky or the same
landscape looks very different to the man of forty
and the man of sixty, and

> " The clouds that gather round the setting sun
> Do take a sober colouring from an eye
> That hath kept watch o'er man's mortality."

Indeed, when we come to close quarters, and
deal with the *fond*—the substance and basis of
my position—I can scarcely persuade myself that
we differ at all ; in fact he more than once con-
firms all I say. My position was, that our cheap
coal was visibly in process of exhaustion, and that
as it became exhausted, our exceptional position
as manufacturers for the whole world must cease,
and that, unless timely emigration saved us, we
should have to meet a crisis of the bitterest suffering and distress. Mr Grant Duff says :—"No
reasonable man doubts that a time will come when
our cheap coal will be exhausted, when we shall,
in all likelihood, cease to be the great workshop of
the world. All I contend for is, that that time is
so far off, that it is idle to speculate at present
about it. Long ere it arrives the whole political
condition of the world may be so entirely altered,
the transference of population from one part of the
globe to another, where it is more wanted, may
be so much a matter of course, that the very word
emigration may have become obsolete, and that
our children may smile as much at the idea of any
mother objecting to her children going to America,
as we now do, when we hear of a mother in Kent
objecting to her children going into the Midland
counties. 'Please God,' said such a one to a

benevolent lady recently, 'no child of mine shall ever go down into the Shires.'"

The paragraph immediately following, has to me a curious ring of being addressed to some such popular constituency, as, in another passage of his paper, he kindly wishes me, as an influence, to keep my political speculations in better order.

"Then I want to know why it should be assumed that the greatness of this country is to be for ever dependent on her manufacturing industry, and on the iron and coal that feed them. That is the present form of our greatness; but we were great before our manufactures, and we will, if we are true to ourselves, be great after them. Coal and iron are but instruments in the hands of that energy which is the true source of our national strength. Coal and iron did not defeat the Armada, did not conquer India, or colonise America."

I seem to have read just the same *ad captandum* phrase in *Punch* the other day :— .

> "Not loss of trade nor failing coal
> This country can disgrace;
> For England's wealth is in the men
> And women of her race."

But what on earth has either piece of self-glorification to do with the argument of mine to which it seems intended as a reply? I said that the *wealth* of England was dependent on her manufacturing industry, and that industry again upon her coal and iron,—a truism if you will, but assuredly not a controvertible proposition ;—and I am met by the "spread-eagleish" reminder that coal and iron are only instruments in the hands of our wonderful energy, that we were great before we had our manufactures, and shall be just as great after we have lost them.   What is this but to maintain that a wealthy and powerful nation will be just as wealthy and powerful (wealth being one of the main elements of power) after it has lost the chief sources of its wealth ; and that a strong man loses nothing of the effectiveness of his strength by having his armour and his weapons taken from him.   Moreover, if a nation's strength and greatness lies in its people *pur et simple*, it must be great just in proportion to the numbers of that people; and a country that by the diminution of its material resources can support only twenty millions, may be as happy and respectable, but can scarcely be as great, as when it maintained thirty millions.   I confess this passage amazed me.   Mr Grant Duff is the furthest possible re-move from either a Philistine or a Yankee.   But does not this sentence (like the subsequent one, wherein he gloats over our enormous national

wealth, and prides himself upon the countless
millions that passed through the clearing-house in
the last year of the Gladstone administration), indicate the unconscious influence which the fact of
representing a Liberal constituency (though perhaps the least Philistinian in the kingdom), exerts
upon a mind not supposed to be especially susceptible to such influences? "We are a great
nation," says the American in *Martin Chuzzlewit*,
"and we must be cracked up."

The more carefully we read Mr Grant Duff's
paper, the more clear, I think, it will appear that,
apart from the very fundamental and pervading difference—that he has, and that I have not, a
liberal constituency in the back-ground to rectify
(or to warp) our respective views,—almost our
only real divergence lies in this—that he has a
blinder confidence in the timely wisdom and the
inherent virtue of both our people and our rulers
than I, regarding the present and reflecting on
the past, am able to feel. He scarcely denies a
single one of the dangers I have signalised; he
only trusts and believes we shall avert them by
calling into operation precisely those agencies
which I carefully specified as the only ones adequate to save us. He admits that "Cassandra

is right in thinking that England cannot remain indefinitely the workshop of the world," but argues that "the adoption of a wise policy" will postpone the evil day, and leave us still in the possession of vast (unspecified) advantages, "which only our unwisdom can take away;" forgetting that this "wise policy" is precisely the questionable postulate. He admits the bad and suicidal character of the trade-union rules and proceedings, but is content to regard them

"As nature's errors on the way to truth,"

which is sanguine, to say the least of it, considering how long they have lasted and how much evil they have wrought. He does not deny —no one knows them better—the tremendous dangers to which we should be exposed were an ill-informed popular electorate to begin to concern themselves with Indian matters; but he is satisfied that they never will so concern themselves enough mischievously to interfere; forgetting that, if it is difficult for demagogues to awaken a steady and enduring *interest* in the affairs of another people, it is only too easy to arouse a sudden passion or a spasmodic sentiment about them, which is noxious just in proportion to its vehemence, its unknowingness, and its transient flame. It is believed by many persons well qualified to form a judgment, that the excitement so recently fanned by the sensational English press, among the sensitive English constituencies, on the late Indian famine, cost this country hard upon five millions sterling, besides sowing the seeds of much probable future mischief; surely not a very hopeful omen for coming times. Finally, Mr Grant Duff's hopes for "parrying the mischiefs which (he admits) must be parried" in order to keep us safe, lie (he tells us) in three things, in "patience" — that is, in waiting till ignorance and folly have exhausted error, and trusting that they will exhaust themselves before it is too late; in "education"—which yet, he says (as I do), must be something very different from what it is now, if it is to prepare men of all classes for the right exercise of their political functions; and in "wise Government"—under which head he proceeds to show how many changes must be made in our policy before it can be considered wise—changes in which I need not follow him, and only very partially agree with him.

Two other very brief comments I have to make before I pass away from this branch of the controversy. Mr Grant Duff observes very truly that our current "divisions into the upper, middle, and lower classes are purely arbitrary, and merely a loose though convenient way of lumping together an immense variety of social strata, which again are laterally divided in innumerable ways."—I am so well aware of this that I carefully avoided these divisions, and spoke of the electorate under two heads, the "propertied class" and the "wage-receiving class"—a classification which I submit is the very reverse of arbitrary, and which, if it cannot be called natural is at least very distinct, very real, and even too permanent and fixed. Again, all my critics, Mr Grant Duff among them, treat the notion of these classes ever pulling together or being unanimous, especially in a crusade against capital, as mere moonshine, "a fear without the ghost of a reason" to justify it. Now, in the first place, this seems to me rather a rash and reckless position to maintain, when not only in this, but in other countries, the most salient social feature of the day is a strife between Labour and Capital (as it is illogically called), more organised, systematic, and persistent, more widely spread and spreading, and in some cases far more bitter than has hitherto been seen ; a strife in which the wage-receiving classes, if they have not shown much sagacity, have at

least shown much unanimity, much power of
united action and endurance. In the second
place, I never supposed, far less predicted, that
the so-called working classes would *as a rule*
gather themselves into one camp, or that they
would not be often divided on political, religious,
and miscellaneous questions. I only pointed out
—and I do not conceive that any one will dispute the proposition—that there *are* questions
which may band them together in one compact
body ; that, when so banded together, our electoral laws will have made them almost irresistible — irresistible at least without a struggle
which we must all contemplate with dismay ;
and that the questions most likely to produce this
ominous union among the classes recently admitted to the franchise are, indisputably, those
connected with the distribution, the acquisition,
and the retention of property. These are the
questions which of all most profoundly interest
the wage-receiving classes—which in their minds
are paramount to all others—on which they are
most likely to hold strong and consentaneous
opinions ; and on which the views of the numerical majority, who possess no property, are most
certain to be at variance with the views of the
educated minority, who possess a great deal.

How any one can dispute these propositions is to me, I confess, inconceivable. How any one can regard the prospect they hold out without uneasiness is, if possible, more inconceivable still.

I am not, and I never was (as Mr Arnold and others seem to suppose) an advocate for withholding political power from "the people," the artizan class, "the masses" if you will. I never believed that full justice would be done, or permanent safety reached, or their interests adequately secured, where they were excluded from all share in the choice of their lawgivers and rulers. I never argued that, as a rule, they were unfit to exercise influence, and a very beneficial influence, on electoral decisions. On the contrary, I have often maintained (and I think I said as much in the paper under discussion) that numbers among them are both morally and intellectually worthier of the franchise than numbers above them in the social scale. And, if it were becoming to be for a moment egotistical, I might say that few men urged earlier or more indefatigably than I schemes for placing on the electoral register every working man who in any way, by any title, according to any rational criterion, was qualified to choose a representative. I anxiously

urged this wise and just conclusion years ago,
when household suffrage was the *anathema
maranatha* of both the political parties who at
last joined in forcing it upon the country. But
certainly I never was in favour of giving to those
masses, whom even their friends designate as
" the residuum," the potential political supremacy
with which Whig and Tory, in 1867, combined
to endow them. I protested against their exclusion just as eagerly as I now protest against their
preponderance. And the impolicy which in 1867
admitted them to the franchise *en bloc* is the
worthy and the natural sequence of the impolicy
which, in the previous five-and-twenty years, refused that franchise to their *élite.*

In nearly all that Mr Grant Duff has written in
reference to my third " Rock Ahead," the religious
one, I cordially concur. Much of it is admir-
able and striking. I only contest the relevancy
of his observations, considered as antagonistic to
the substance of my thesis. No doubt the religious
sentiment, and much of the religious creed, of
truly pious and highly spiritual natures, being
matter of intuitive conviction and consciousness
of communion with God, will survive the destruc-
tion of " evidences " and the disproof of dogmas

of detail ;—but what proportion of the religion of
ordinary English men and women is of this lofty
and genuinely personal type? No doubt, again,
the criticisms, the researches, the analyses, the
logic, which are shaking to their very core the old
and current creeds—the doctrines of the prayer-
book and the articles and the formularies of all
Christian sects—do not assail, do not even touch
or approach, "the reverential feelings and beliefs of
the higher forms of Christianity." I said as much
myself, and put forth an aspiration that this
higher and purified form might in time become
the adopted religion of our teachers and our people.
But no one knows better than my critic, that the
religion, the faith, the Christianity, of nine-tenths
of those, who in this country are still believers, is
not of this nobler and robuster sort, and has little
of this vein of inward and unassailable conviction;
—that, on the contrary, it rests mainly (where
it can properly be said to rest upon anything at
all beyond mere habit, and the prevalent opinions
of those around them), upon the *assumptions* of
the inspiration of the Scriptures, the reality of the
miracles of the New Testament, and the supposition that the Gospels are narratives by four
independent eye-witnesses of the transactions they
relate ;—that all these articles of belief are now

rudely shaken, if not altogether disproved in the minds of most thinking persons ;—and that it is at least probable that, with the undermining or removal of the foundation, the edifice itself must crumble. It may be the fault of churches and divines that so essential an element of high national life as Christianity should have been built up on such a sandy ground:—rather, I would say, it is their fault to have made our national Christianity such a system of mysteries, and dogmas, and impossible statements, and unintelligible scholasticisms as only the fundamental assumptions above enumerated could sustain ;. but, still, such our national Christianity is, and has been made,—and being such, I affirm that every year it stands in greater and greater peril of being abandoned or swept away, as every year, by sure, steady, hastening, advances, the searching inquiries of our bold modern thought are perceptibly sapping its base.

It is true, no doubt, as Mr Grant Duff eloquently maintains, that true Christian principles and sentiments never had so wide a public influence in Europe, and in England, as just at this moment when I represent Christianity as in such danger of being discarded.

"At no previous period in the history of the

world has Christianity, as represented in the
gospels, or in the lives and works of the best of
its followers, exercised so powerful an influence
on public affairs as in the last thirty years ; and I
make this assertion without in the least forgetting
the endless wars and troubles of that period.

" In legislation, in administration, in our way of
carrying on war, in our treatment of inferior races,
in our social relations, in our amusements, in our
literature, in everything we are though, Heaven
knows, still far enough from it, nearer nevertheless to the Christian ideal than we ever have been
before ; and it is interesting to observe that the
results of the very highest statesmanship and of
the very highest forms of Christianity are often
most curiously near each other.

" If Christianity is going to lose its power at
once over the highest intelligence of Western
Europe and over the masses, just as it seems to be
making itself more really felt in public affairs than
it ever was in the so-called Ages of Faith, the
course of this world is certainly the maddest piece
of business.   I confess, however, I do not believe
one syllable of any such prophecy.   The words
once spoken amongst the Syrian hills will never
lose their echo.   The saying falsely attributed to

Julian is profoundly true, ' O Galilean ! thou hast conquered !' "

That prophecy, I beg to say, was not mine. I never said that the Christianity which has done all these great things and exercised this wide influence for good—" *Christianity as represented in the gospels, and in the lives and works of its best followers*"—is losing its hold over the highest intelligence or the masses of Great Britain. It is not the dogmatic Christian creed, as taught in our churches and chapels, that has wrought these marvels, and is still working so powerfully for progress ; it is the spirit, the temper, the morality of Christ, which those incongruous dogmas and that incrusting creed have never, thank God! been able wholly to smother or disguise, and which, if theologians permit, will survive their overthrow. I, too, believe that "the Galilean has conquered," and will conquer ; but it will be the true Galilean of history, not the travestied Galilean of Nicene or Athanasian formularies, of sacraments and sacerdotalism, of miracles and mysteries and legends, and everlasting torments for all who cannot believe the unbelievable.

But why do we waste words in a purely imaginary controversy? Mr Grant Duff evidently believes just as I do, that the current Christianity

of the average Englishman must crumble to pieces
before the pure faith of Jesus can emerge out of
its ruins. " The time for reconstructing the religious thought of Europe," he thinks, "lies far
ahead, in a happier age than ours. The dissolvent
process must go far further, and elements not
thought of now must be considered before the
process of theoretical reconstruction can begin."
Like me, too,—though in far more vigorous words,
—he condemns, " as the worst antichrists of our
time, the bungling sophists who denounce science
and historical criticism, because they do not square
with the vile little systems which they, and others
like them, have built on Christ's immortal words,
—who yelp at our modern masters of those who
know."

I.

POLITICAL ROCK.

I.

THE part of Cassandra can never be a pleasant one for any man to play. It makes others uncomfortable and himself unpopular. It is always annoying both to individuals and nations to be warned, with irritating pertinacity and lucidity still more exasperating, of dangers imminent or future which may be unavoidable, and which will probably be fatal if not averted. The more unanswerable the prophet, the more hated he is sure to be, and the more neglected he is likely to be. People detest, and usually resent, being told of impending peril or catastrophe, especially if they see no remedy and no escape, and if the menaced ruin can be laid at no door but their own.

Yet this unwelcome and ungrateful part is sometimes the only one left to the lover of his country, and one from which, if the love be true, he will not shrink. In modern days, too, the condition of a nation, advanced in civilization, still sound at the core, and full of citizens at once wise and faithful, can

A

seldom be so absolutely hopeless as to warrant those
who foresee dangers in taking refuge in a lazy, timid,
or selfish silence. The recuperative power latent in
a nation blessed with free institutions, an historic
past, and a numerous leisure and highly educated
class, must always be very great. To the last it
must be the duty of the look-out man at the mast-
head to warn the steersman of the shoals and breakers
he discerns, though the steersman may refuse to put
up the helm, or the ship may have too much way
upon her to be checked or turned aside in time. If
the vessel of the State profit by the warning, the
effort and the obloquy will be of small account indeed.
If not, the saddened and unheeded patriot will quit
the scene of his failure with the less regret.

> Lubenter quiesceremus libertate partâ;
> Quiescimus, amissâ, perlubenter.*

"Willingly would we have died to liberate our
country—not having been able to liberate her, we die
still more willingly."

Now, it is my conviction that there are three
especial dangers hanging over the future of England
—three " Rocks ahead " on which the dignity and
well-being of the country and the happiness of its
citizens may not improbably be wrecked. They may
be distant, yet perhaps not very distant, for they are

---

* Walter Savage Landor's epitaph on the defeated Spanish
Patriots; quoted in " St Clement's Eve," by Sir Henry Taylor.

distinctly visible to an observant and forecasting mind.
People in general think little of them, or scarcely
believe in them, because they do not as yet *force*
themselves upon the vision.   We are a busy race and
much engrossed with the present hour; Englishmen
never did look far before them, too occupied with the
cares and needs of to-day to take anxious heed for
to-morrow—still less to speculate on the pregnant
possibilities of the day after : we are a sanguine race,
moreover, and prone to trust that "something is
certain to turn up" to save us from what we dislike
or dread ; and, in spite of our political instincts and
practical training, we have an astonishing faculty for
sowing seeds of the most surely germinating and
prolific sort, without actually realizing in our own
minds that, in the fullness of time, they must ripen
to an inevitable harvest, and without any grave consideration as to what sort of a crop we shall then be
called upon to reap.   I wish, therefore, not only to
signalize those dangers which I seem to see coming,
but to force my countrymen to look them in the face,
however unpleasant the sight may be; to decide
whether they are real or imaginary, and, if the
former, how they may be met, mitigated, or averted.

The three national dangers I allude to, to state
them very broadly, are—

    I. The political supremacy of the lower classes.

    II. The approaching industrial decline of England.

    III. The divorce of the Intelligence of the country
        from its Religion.

There exist, no doubt, many minor perils, but these are vital;—and of these the first is *political*, the second *economical*, the third *intellectual* and *moral;* and all of them may be termed *social* in a serious degree. In dealing with them I will endeavour most sedulously to state no facts or premises that are doubtful, and to draw no inferences that can be controverted; so that no question can arise as to my conclusions unless new elements or opposing influences are called into existence to overthrow the calculation.

I. If an orator or historian were to speak of " The Revolution of 1867," few would understand what he meant; and as soon as he was understood, nearly every one would charge him with extravagance and hyperbole. Yet in that year a transformation was effected in the political constitution of these islands, so complete and ˌthorough that few revolutions in modern times have been more sweeping. But because it was wrought with customary legal forms— because the process was accompanied by no bloodshed, no violence, no disturbance even, and but small excitement—because there was no change of dynasty —and most of all, perhaps, because the transformation, though total, was gradual and not sudden, we have ·failed to recognize its revolutionary character. The medicine—or the poison—may be slow to operate; but, once taken, the ultimate effect is certain; and in this case there is no antidote known to the political Pharmacopœia.

The Revolution we speak of consists in this. The Reform Bill of 1867 takes the command of the representation out of the hands of the propertied classes, and puts it into the hands of the wage-receiving classes. It gives it over from the upper and middle ranks of the community to the lower ranks. It transfers electoral preponderance — that is, in fact, electoral supremacy — from property to proletairism, from capital to labour. And it does this not one whit the less undeniably and irretrievably, in that it does it (thus far) only potentially and prospectively. It does it in virtue of three provisions—household suffrage in boroughs, household suffrage in counties, and vote by ballot,—the first and last are *faits accomplis;* the second has been announced by the chiefs of both parties as forthcoming to complete the edifice. Now, in round numbers the population of this kingdom may be divided into *eight* millions of persons who hold realized property of some sort, and *twenty-four* millions of persons who hold no property, but subsist by the labour of their hands. These twenty-four millions, or the householders among them, who may be reckoned at one-fifth—have now votes, or will have very shortly, or may have when they please; and they *can,* therefore, when they please, outvote and overpower the householders among the eight millions, who may be reckoned at one-fourth. That is, to put it broadly, there are or may be, and soon will be, *five* millions poor electors against *two* millions of well-to-do electors;—and each vote of one class counts for just as much as each vote of the other. It is idle to argue that the working classes will not pull together, nor the poor be thus in a mass arrayed against the rich :—probably not yet ; possibly not as a rule ; almost certainly not except on class questions of a social character.* But sometimes they will, and at any time they may ; and the broad indisputable fact remains that the lower class of voters are far the most numerous; are, or may be, preponderant in the proportion of five to two or five to three ; and that in consequence when they are all registered and whenever they choose to draw together, they will be despotic at the poll, and have the command of the representation in the House of Commons. Now, the House of Commons, as we all know, is all but omnipotent.

But this is not all. These poorer voters may be

---

* *Audi alteram partem.* I quote the views of a kindly critic in the *Scotsman*,—Mr Greg says—" It is idle to argue that the working classes will not pull together, nor the poor be thus in a mass pitted against the rich." We are not so sure of the idleness of such an argument. There is this in its favour, that, not even in the most democratic countries in the world, has there ever been anything that could be called a union of the masses against property—of the have nots against the haves. And there are reasons against concluding that what has not been seen in the past of any country will be seen in the future of ours. Those who are called "the poor" or "the working classes" are really not one class, but several classes, with various degrees of intelligence, with various interests, and even with various ranks. There is less of sympathy, of a sense of common interest, or even of mutual respect, between the upper and lower strata of the working classes—between, say, a skilled and intelligent artisan and an ignorant and half-pauper

not only preponderant, but supreme. They may name not only *three-fifths* of the members, but nearly *the whole of them.* They may absolutely exclude those whom they outnumber at the polling booths from any share whatever in the representation. Nay, more ; unless we have a supplementary and most decisively intelligent Reform Bill, they will assuredly do this. Only the " cumulative vote," or universal " three-cornered constituencies," or Mr Hare's plan, or some of the wise, but utterly disregarded suggestions of Lord Grey, can avert the probability of this extreme result. The operation of our unscientific and undiscerning system of representation enables the party which preponderates in any constituency, even by a minute fraction, to monopolize all the members ; while it is only the extremely heterogeneous character of our electoral divisions (a characteristic which will

---

labourer—than there is between several of the higher strata of those who are thus spoken of as one class, and some of the strata of those spoken of as another and dissimilar class. Such differences in position, feeling, and real or supposed interests, exist not only as between the extremes, but through all the gradations of those Mr Greg speaks of as " the working classes." One who knew them well, and also loved them well, wrote of them, and not reproachfully—" Tenpenny Jim sneers at Ninepenny Joe ; " and that expresses an important truth. Many recent events, too, must have helped to teach them that that instinct is well grounded which leads them to disbelieve that they have a common interest, and especially an interest apart from the interests of the other classes of the community—for instance, the rise in miners' wages has been severely felt at the hearth of working men of every other employment: the gain of one section of the working class has been a heavy loss to the class in general.

not long survive unmodified) which prevents this anomalous and inequitable result from extending to the whole country. If we ever have equal and *similar* electoral districts, the barest majority of the nation may become not only *preponderant* in the House of Commons (which is right), but *omnipotent* and *absolute* (which would be iniquitous and monstrous). It is, therefore, always on the cards that the lower classes *might* not only overpower opposition and discussion, but absolutely *exclude* both.

We are warranted in calling this state of affairs " revolutionary "—not only because it is startling, but because it is altogether new ; and this point demands special attention. We have had " Representative Institutions " for a score of generations. We have never had " Popular Representation," as Transatlantic and Continental nations understand it,—that is, *the representation of the numerical majority*—till now. We have inaugurated an entirely novel and untried experiment, in prognosticating the working and results of which the Past can be no guide whatever. The reform may have been just, may have been wise, may have been unavoidable—as to these questions opinions differ, and we need not discuss them. But there can be no difference as to the fact that the change is not a carrying out, a completion, a perfectation of our former system, but a reversal of it ;—that we have not " crowned the edifice," but rebuilt it in a different style and on a fresh foundation. It is curious that so undeniable a truth should have been so little realised or dwelt upon. So far as I know the only concise statement of it appeared in the " Quarterly Review " a couple of years ago :—

" Previous to 1832,—in those old times when England was so great and paramount a nation, when we were so proud of our institutions, when we were so exceptionally free,—Representation was not a reality in the sense in which we have made it so now. Classes were represented ; property was represented ; education was represented ; guilds—*i.e.*, industries, were represented ; but individuals, numbers, the masses of the people, were not. The House of Commons pictured and reproduced the nation in a sort of general and often faithful fashion,—that is, it shared and reflected the opinion of the important, motive, influential classes of the community ; but popular representation, in the sense in which it is now understood and carried out, —in which Rousseau and Sièyes understood it, in which France and America understand it,—did not exist. It was prevented from existing by four things :—By the limited suffrage, which gave votes only to proprietors, leaseholders, burghers, freemen, and graduates ; by close and rotten boroughs, which gave members to extinct towns, and refused them to thriving cities ; by the influence of peers and landed proprietors, which practically placed the votes of the tenants at the disposal of their landlords ; and by party management, which largely over-rode individual preferences. That representative system, which we were so proud of, which answered so well in the past (illogical and bristling with anomalies as it was), which surrounding nations admired and envied, and fancied they were going to imitate, has been swept away. What we have installed now, under the same name, is something wholly different, something quite new, something as yet untried and problematic. It is no more the same thing, than Mr John Smith the manufacturer is of the same family as Mr Algernon Sydney, the extinct feudal gentleman, because he has purchased his estate and lives in his ancestral manor-house ; nor can it be any more expected to act in the same way. In fine, we hitherto have lived under representative institutions *nominally* only,—that is, under such restraints, modifications, inconsistencies, almost denials, as made them yield most of their good and little of their evil operation. Other nations have lived under them *really*, in their bald and naked truthfulness, and we are now about to do the same. The 'sham '—to speak broadly—did succeed with us on the whole wonderfully. Will the actuality succeed as well ? We cannot tell, and have no desire to vaticinate ; as yet we have only foreign analogies, always imperfect, to guide our conjecture. Certainly, unrestricted suffrage, thoroughly popular representation, cannot be said to have succeeded—indeed may be said to have deplorably failed— in France and the United States. During the Restoration, from 1815 to 1847, Parliamentary Government worked fairly in France : so it did in America up to about forty or fifty years ago ; so it did in Switzerland till a generation since ; so it does in Italy at present. But in all these cases, and up to these dates, they had kept clear of anything like Universal Suffrage. In France, under Louis XVIII. and Louis Philippe, the electors scarcely exceeded 250,000, and there were nearly 600,000 Government appointments to divide among them. In Italy, the franchise qualification is not high, but the entire constituent body scarcely reaches a quarter of a million. In Prussia, all men have votes, or nearly so ; but there the thoroughly anti-democratic system of double election is in practice."

Who, then, and what, are the classes to whom we

have thus undeniably handed over electioneering preponderance—that is, the supreme political power in the State in ultimate resort ? For that those classes, the numerical majority in the country, do possess this power and preponderance *potentially*, and may possess it, and are nearly certain ere long to possess it *actually*, and are already assuming it *gradually*,* is not to be disguised by the fact that they have not as yet fully realised or greedily taken up their inheritance. It is there waiting for them whenever they choose to qualify and register ; and their leaders will not let many years elapse before they have stirred them up to do this. The numerical majority are henceforth virtually our masters ; will not *be*, but will nominate, sway, indoctrinate, or rather inoculate, our

---

* We have no recent returns to guide us in determining the actual numbers of the wage-receiving classes already on the register, but the following comparison may afford some intimation It would seem as if Mr Disraeli's Reform Bill had more than doubled the number of electors in England and Wales, who now amount to 2,156,000, or about 40 per cent. of the adult males. The Reform Bill of 1832 only added 54 per cent. in 30 years. The Reform Bill of 1867 has added upwards of 100 per cent. in five years.

ELECTORS IN ENGLAND AND WALES.

	1832-3.	1862-3.	1869.	1873.
Counties	370,000	534,000	792,000	801,000
Boroughs	285,000	478,000	1,203,000	1,356,000
Total	655,000	1,012,000	1,995,000	2,157,000

A later return for 1874 gives the total electors for England and Wales at 2,245,108, and for the United Kingdom, 2,764,285.

Household suffrage for the counties will in time add probably half a million to the rural constituencies.

rulers; and the numerical majority consist, and to all appearance will long consist, of the wage-receiving classes, of those who depend on weekly earnings, and live in an overwhelming proportion by the labour of their hands. Now, what will be in the main their party predilections, whether Tories or Liberals most possess or are most likely to win their support, is a question which concerns us little. The essential point at issue is whether they are fit, or can be made fit, to exercise righteously and wisely the responsible duties imposed upon them by the power which has been given to them. Without echoing for a moment—indeed, while repudiating with infinite disgust—the insincere flattery which has been heaped upon them by candidates of all colours, we may fairly admit that the working-classes of this country are on the whole more intelligent, more fair, more sober-minded, and, but for their drinking pro-pensities, more respectable than those of most other lands. They are, we believe, sound at heart—they are not envious, and they are as a rule both energetic, industrious, and of an independent spirit. Properly trained, properly led, properly dealt with, we are satisfied they would make out and out the best Proletariat in the world. Our only charge against them in regard to our present topic is that, labouring with their hands from morning to night, and living from hand to mouth, they are not (perhaps) necessarily *very* poor or *very* ignorant, but necessarily the *most* ignorant as well as the poorest, because the least instructed and the least leisurely of all sections of the community. They are not perhaps actually or always the worst off, but they often feel themselves to be so, and may easily be represented to themselves as being so. They are not, we suspect, the most discontented class; but it is to their credit that they are not so, and there are not wanting orators and agitators who seek incessantly to make them so. At all events, they are the least richly provided with the good things of this life, and *inevitably* the most poorly endowed with political knowledge while the most amply endowed with political power. They are not a whit more selfish than other classes—indeed they are often more generous and high-minded than the class immediately above them; * they are not a whit

---

* The following were among the latest utterances of perhaps the wisest, fairest, and most candid Radical of our times—Mr Grote: "I have outlived," he said, "three great illusions. First, I always held that if supreme power were held by the people, it would be exercised more righteously than when entrusted to one person or a few. But this I have now found to be a mistake. Secondly, I always maintained that Ireland might be made contented and loyal by governing her in the same way as England, and for that reason I constantly opposed, when in Parliament, the enactment of Coercion Bills, and all exceptional legislation in reference to the sister kingdom. But I grieve to say that I have now come to a different conclusion. Thirdly, I cherished the persuasion that as the people advanced in intelligence and material prosperity, they would esteem it a duty and a privilege to educate their own children, without invoking the assistance of the State or any other body. But this I find to be the greatest delusion of all, and I must add that the rich have done their best to instil into the people the notion that the education of their children belongs to others.

less honest or probably less fair ; they are simply less educated, less sagacious, and less well-informed ; and, therefore, obviously less competent to decide political questions, to choose political guides, to wield political power. And they are all this from no fault that we can reproach them with, but from the nature of the case,—because from the cradle to the grave they have less leisure and fewer advantages for knowledge, reflection, and mental discipline.

" I have outlived my faith in the efficacy of Republican govern=ment regarded as a check upon the vulgar passions of a majority in a nation, and I recognise the fact that supreme power lodged in their hands *may* be exercised quite as mischievously as by a despotic ruler like the First Napoleon. The conduct of the Northern States, in the late conflict with the Southern States, has led me to this conclusion, though it cost me much to avow it, even to myself.

" I have come to perceive that the choice between one man and another, among the English people, signifies less than I used formerly to think it did. Take a section of society, cut it through from top to bottom, and examine the composition of the succes-sive layers. They are much alike throughout the scale. The opinions, all based upon the same social instincts : never upon a clear or enlightened perception of *general interests.* Every particular class pursuing its own, the result is, a universal struggle for the advantages accruing from *party* supremacy. The English mind is much of one pattern, take whatsoever class you will. The same favourite prejudices, amiable and otherwise ; the same antipathies, coupled with ill-regulated, though benevolent efforts to eradicate human evils, are well-nigh universal : modified naturally, by instruction, among the highly educated few : but *they* hardly affect the course of out-of-doors sentiment. I believe, therefore, that the actual composition of Parliament represents with tolerable fidelity the British people. And it will never be better than it is, for a House of Commons *cannot afford to be above its own constituencies in knowledge or patriotism.*"

No one can deny the strict accuracy of the statement. No one can be blind to the manifest dangers of the position. The science of government is never a simple one even in the best and easiest of times. In modern days, " Society "—" the State "—has become strangely, almost fearfully complex, influenced by a hundred causes, encompassed by a hundred perils, wrought upon by a hundred agencies—often slow in their operation, often hidden in their sources, often difficult of discovery even by the trained eye, often difficult of estimation even by the instructed mind. The welfare, even the safety, of a community like ours depends upon the thorough comprehension of a multitude of concurrent or conflicting influences, some economical, some moral, some legal, which would task any ability and any experience ; years of discipline and study are barely sufficient for the work, as those feel most who have watched it closest ; it demands, as we habitually recognise (in words at least), *the best wisdom* and the *best virtue* of the nation. How is this best wisdom and best virtue to be discerned, selected, and preferred, by the especially unthinking and uninformed ? Grant that the masses will honestly desire to choose the best and the wisest men to rule them, by what test can they possibly discover them ? by what instinct can they possibly appreciate them ? The very depth of a true statesman's sagacity, the very forecast of a true statesman's vision, will alienate from him the sympathies of the average elector. The very fact of the states-

man seeing farther than the elector, will make him
seem to the elector to see wrong. We can all guess
what would happen in war were the common soldiers
to choose their generals. Yet government is a more
complicated affair than war ; and the common soldier
has at least a professional training, which the prole-
tarian householder has not.

But to stop at these general propositions would be
to take a very inadequate and unimpressive view of
the specific dangers which surround us. Let us come
a little closer to the facts of the case. Our House of
Commons is composed of a number of politicians
eagerly competing for the suffrages of uninstructed
and toiling men—mostly poor, sometimes suffering
under a sense of wrong, often groaning and sinking
under the burden of labour and care. These men
understand nothing of the art of government, nothing
of economic science, nothing of policy in general. But
they have a lively sense of their own wants, and a
strong feeling of their own grievances. They naturally
wish to mend their own condition and redress what
seem to be their wrongs ; they wish this more vehemently than anything else ; and they have no notion
of not using their electoral power to achieve these
objects ; naturally, therefore, they will be prone to
give their votes to those who engage to promote these
objects. That is, their favoured candidates will as a
rule be those who most fall in with their ideas, share
or flatter their prejudices, promise to work for their
interests. Now, what are the objects which the working men, the wage-receiving classes, have notoriously

and inevitably most at heart—must have most at heart—cannot for a moment be blamed for having most at heart? Clearly, higher wages, shorter hours, more power of dictating conditions of work, and less strictness in the interpretation of contracts;—and all these things *more or less directly through the instru-mentality of legislation.* They wish for two other things beside,—relief from all taxation which in any way increases the cost of living, and increase in those sorts of public expenditure which create a demand for their labour. Now, in all this there is no ground for reproach to them, but much ground for apprehending danger to the country. There is no ground for reproach to them, because it is inevitable that unedu-cated men should be more swayed by personal interests than by political considerations; * they understand, or fancy they understand, the one—they do not under-stand, and usually do not pretend or aspire to under-stand, the other; the first touch them very closely— the second only remotely and intermediately; indeed, the very highest species of training is required (a training at once intellectual and moral) to recognise in the first place that the interests of each class must be postponed to the general well-being of the com-

* "The difference between an arbitrary and a limited monarchy vanishes, when compared with the difference between one meal a day and three meals a day. It is a poor consolation to a man who has had no breakfast, and expects no supper, that the king does not possess a dispensing power, and that troops cannot be raised in time of peace without the consent of Parliament."— *Edinburgh Review,* June, 1827.

munity; in the second place, that these interests are
in the end best served through the community being
well organised and governed in the interests of all;
and in the third place, that nearly all evils and grievances complained of are to be remedied, not by a
Parliamentary decree that they shall cease, but by a
careful and searching diagnosis, by a patient investigation of the often remote causes, economic or other, in
which they have their source.   The more uninstructed
and unintelligent an electorate is, the more will it regard special and individual objects and interests in
preference to questions of general policy; the less
able will it be to perceive how general policy bears
upon particular interests; the more prone will it be
to attack evils and grievances in their symptoms
rather than in their sources; and to insist on their
immediate removal without any power of perceiving
or any disposition to consider the secondary consequences, however mischievous, which may result from
their removal.   Now, the *average* intellectual training
and capacity of our constituencies is lowering year by
year, and must be lowering continuously, as larger
and larger numbers of the more ignorant class of
householders are placed upon the register (unless, indeed, education should advance faster than constituencies swell), and the standard of representative
intelligence will naturally lower also, though it may
be more gradually and at a considerable interval.*

* I am not disposed to under-estimate the political education of
our constituencies through the process of the electoral speeches

Higher wages, indeed, we do not suppose will be sought through direct legislative action : but shorter hours (which practically mean, or are designed to mean, higher wages) will be, and, as we all know, are so sought ; and sought, too, without any perception of the inevitable consequence—*viz.*, that the cost of production becomes enhanced as labour grows less productive ; that the price of articles rises, and living becomes more expensive, as house-rent is swollen by combinations in the building trades, and by combinations among colliers, and so on. Power on the part of operatives to dictate conditions of work to their employers by threatened strikes and Trade Union regulations is already sought directly by legislative enactment and legislative repeal, with entire blindness to the remote effect of those measures in ultimately placing British industry at a disadvantage with that of other countries where similar interferences are not permitted. The mischief will be done blindly— in ignorance, not with ill intention ; but when once

---

made to them in such abundance by their members or the candidates who seek their suffrages. Experienced politicians, I know, speak of the progress and influence of this species of instruction as astonishing and re-assuring. Still the fact remains that the classes brought under this kind of instruction as the suffrage lowers are the least able to profit by it, from want of previous educational preparation. The symptom, no doubt, is a hopeful set-off against gloomier prognostics ; but it must be remembered that it is only the electioneering speeches of candidates decidedly above the average in wisdom, honesty, and independence, that can truly educate a constituency, and that the number of such candidates is likely to fall off year by year.

done will be irreparable, and (as I intend to show in the next section) the result may be something nearer ruin than mere calamity. And how can it be expected that a Legislature preponderatingly selected by working men, or a Government appointed by that Legislature, will be firm in resisting the unwise demands or repressing the immoral violence and disorders of working men ?—that is, in controlling the special errors and dangers into which the majority of their constituents, their masters and creators, are most prone to fall ? The relief of the wage-receiving classes from taxation has already been inaugurated, and for many years has been steadily progressing; the tendency is not to be regretted, and we are by no means inclined to pronounce that as yet it has been pushed too far. The necessaries of life have long been exempted from all fiscal contributions; taxes upon articles of general consumption, which may be termed the poor man's luxuries, such as coffee, tea, and sugar, have been repeatedly and largely reduced; and " a free breakfast-table," whenever achieved, will have completed his exemption. The liquor-tax will be the only one he will still be called upon to pay; and that is so far voluntary that he may pretty much regulate it for himself. The crusade against indirect taxation—the only taxation that *can* ever practically be levied on the wage-receiving classes * — in our

---

* Some fiscal authorities, we are aware, dream of levying a stamp-tax on wages; but no employers of labour, or persons qualified by experience to form an opinion, will endorse the impracticable scheme.

judgment a shortsighted, inequitable, and pernicious
crusade—is supported by too many respected names
in the political world for its success not to be highly
probable, to say the least ; and when a Legislature
chosen in the main by working men, shall have
relieved their principal constituents from all contribu-
tion to the revenue, what prospect will there be of
economy in the outlay of that revenue, which must
be in so large a measure spent in the employment of
labour? Taxation, levied exclusively on tne rich, and
expended mainly in subsidising or employing the
poor, is certain to be lavish and oppressive, when the
classes who vote it and profit by it pay no portion of
it—or human nature would not be what it is.

Again, to advert to questions more strictly political, what would be the prospects of our Indian
Empire if ever the English masses began to interest
themselves upon the subject, and to attempt to form,
and fancy themselves competent to form, an opinion
upon the score or two of difficult and complicated
matters connected with that anomalous dependency
which are constantly cropping up for decision,—each
requiring thorough acquaintance with the peculiar
condition, surroundings, and characteristics of a
wholly alien race ? Is it not a daily matter for
congratulation on the part of every experienced and
qualified statesman, with scarcely an exception, that
Parliament has hitherto taken so rare and so faint an
interest in Indian questions—that their management
has virtually been left to men who can appreciate the

marvellously delicate handling they require ? Even
with the actual House of Commons, if every member
believed himself as competent to help to govern India
as he does to govern Ireland, and made it as habitual
a topic for discussion and for party controversy, how
long could we retain our hold, or maintain there that
" Roman Peace," which, amid all our mistakes, has
proved so signal a blessing to the heterogeneous
nations and classes which we overrule ? But if that
House of Commons were elected by still more ignorant constituencies—constituencies unaware of their
ignorance precisely in proportion to its totality—and
peculiarly liable, in consequence of that very ignorance, to be excited and misled by any fanatical de-
claimer, would not the extra difficulty, the extra cost,
the extra danger, become something passing calculation ? Or, in the domain of foreign policy, if we had
a House of Commons dependent on the suffrages and
reflecting the sentiments of uneducated and therefore
susceptible millions, of good impulses probably, but of
the most superficial views, and utterly unskilled to
comprehend hidden connections or foresee secondary
results—without the first rudiments of absolutely
indispensable information,—how long could we stave
off Continental or Transatlantic hostilities, or those
" strained relations " which are almost as noxious as
actual war ? Fancy a Foreign Policy, dictated by
an ignorant democracy—usually almost asleep, sometimes waking frantically—paying no taxes, yet dispos-
ing of a vast revenue levied upon others—and inspired

with an absolute conviction alike in the righteousness
of their cause and the supremacy of their strength !

In writing as we have done, have we mis-stated or
over-stated a single fact, or drawn a single questionable inference ?   Are not the wage-receiving classes
potentially already, and about to be *actually*, ere
long, the majority of the electoral body ?   Must they
not ultimately—can they not whenever they please—
predominate at the Poll in the ratio of at least five to
three ?   Must they not—however good, however improved, however well-intentioned as a rule—always,
from the necessity of the case, constitute the *least*
instructed, the *least* intelligent, the *least* leisurely, if
not also the least contented portion of the community;
and therefore *the least competent to judge political
questions or to choose political guides and rulers ?*
Are not foreign questions and Indian questions almost
absolutely and inevitably out of their range of capacity
—though alas ! it may be feared, not out of their
reach of interference ?   Are they not certain, in the
main, to be swayed rather by urgent class interests,
windy fanaticisms, and hasty passions, than by wide
principles of public policy ?   Must not a general
lowering and vulgarizing of the maxims of our legislation and administration, and of the character of
our statesmen and politicians, be the almost inevitable
result ?   Is it not consonant to all experience that,
having preponderating power, they, like others, will
use and direct that power towards the promotion of
their own fancied interests rather than towards the

general good—which, indeed, they will not be qualified
thoroughly to estimate ? Is it not more than probable
that in pursuit of this end, they will, from sheer want
of knowledge, foresight, and intelligence, fall into
economical and political blunders which may be fatal
to their own cause, though the fatality may not be
discovered in time ? And may it not be predicted
with nearly absolute confidence that, having on various
plausible pleas—plausible enough really to deceive
and satisfy willing minds—relieved their own class
from all fiscal burdens, the public expenditure   (little
of which will be drawn from them, and most of which
will be divided among them), will undergo marvellous
inflation ? Men of property will pay the taxes, while
labouring men will vote them and determine how they
shall be spent. It appears to me that not one of
these questions can be answered in the negative ;—
and that the sum-total is rather appalling.

"But," it will be replied, "all these gloomy prognostics assume that we are dealing with an uneducated
population, and our people will soon be no longer so.
We are taking Mr. Lowe's advice, and have set to
work in earnest to 'educate our masters.'"—Build no
sanguine hopes of escaping the Rock ahead on a delusion
such as this. Instruction, such as we are giving, can
do little, and comes too late. As has been truly said:—

"We have given the masses power *suddenly ;* we are
giving them education only *by slow degrees.* We have

given them *much* power: we can give them only *little* education. Nay: we give them *supreme* power, with at best a most *superficial* and probably *transient* education. Finally, we give the power to the *existing* generation; we propose to educate the *next*. We give the votes on which are to turn, and may at any crisis turn, the destinies of the country, to the untrained adults between twenty-one and seventy-five years of age; we *intend to train* in the capacity to know how to vote the children between six and fourteen. And we plume ourselves upon being a just and sagacious, and above all a ' practical ' nation !

" But this is not all. *Can* we ' educate our masters ? ' What sort and amount of that education which alone could fit them to understand political questions, to decide in political difficulties, to choose between political candidates and guides, can we bestow upon them ? The great mass of them must go forth to earn their own living at the age of thirteen or fourteen, and toil hard ever after. The mere rudiments of knowledge are, therefore, all that can be drilled into them at any school. The larger number will have learned to read and write imperfectly, and will soon lose even that imperfect acquisition. A certain percentage will learn to write well, to read with fluency and ease, to take pleasure in what they have acquired, and will probably retain much of it, and take what opportunities fall in their way afterwards of adding to it. But is that an education which will render them competent to exercise the electoral franchise with discretion ; to distinguish the demagogue from the statesman ; to detect the nonsense of the popular fallacy, and the insincerity or ignorance of the fluent tribune; to turn away from the plausible socialistic delusion, and pounce upon and hold fast the dry economic truth ? In short, is it possible—by any kind or degree of school training which is within reach or can be brought within

reach of those who, from the age of fourteen onward, must
be striving toilsomely for their daily bread—to make them
as competent to choose good representatives, to support wise
rulers, and to insist upon sound measures of legislation and
administration, as those from whom you have taken the
prepotent voice in these matters ?"

It is simply discreditable to deceive ourselves as we
are trying to do in this great matter, and it may be
fatal. It may be at once admitted that the style and
standard of the education given at our primary schools
—the only ones attended, or that probably as a rule
ever will be attended, by the great body of the
labouring class—is improving slowly year ·by year.
It is confidently hoped that ere long nearly the entire
population will be passed through those schools. But
when that is done, what does it all mean ? The facts
on which our attention has to be fixed are these.
First, that above two-thirds of the children " leave
school at ten years of age, and learn nothing more as
long as they live ;" *secondly,* that, as a general fact,
those alone who remain till thirteen or fourteen, and
reach " the fourth standard," retain in after life what
they have acquired, and that the number who remain
thus long and reach this standard is only an insignificant fraction of the whole ; and *thirdly,* that the
" sixth standard," which scarcely any attain, is the
lowest which embodies the degree or character of
education requisite to qualify its recipient to continue
his training for himself in after-life, or to judge fitly
of the political considerations which come before a

Parliamentary elector.* "It is obvious" (writes one Inspector—and we believe all his colleagues would agree with him) "that unless a child can show an amount of knowledge something like the higher standards of the Code, he holds out very meagre promise that any permanent effect will follow from his school career." Mr Mundella told the House of Commons, in March 1870, "that the English sixth standard (Revised Code), *our highest,* is below the lowest Saxon, Prussian, or Swiss standard, even for country schools. We had never yet passed 20,000 in a population of 20,000,000 to the sixth standard in one year; whereas Old Prussia (without her recent aggrandisement) passed nearly 380,000 every year." Dr Lyon Playfair might well say :—"What we call education in the inspected schools of England is the mere seed used in other countries; but with us that

---

* The figures for 1872 are these for England and Wales, in primary schools :

Total numbers of children between 6 and 13 years, or 8 and 15 years (about) 3,600,000, of whom belonging to the classes in question probably 2,700,000
Number in average attendance at school . . 1,336,000
„ examined 661,600
„ examined in Standards IV. to VI. . 118,800
„ passed 68,800

That is, of the total number who ought to have been at school, only 50 per cent. were actually under instruction; of the number instructed only 50 per cent. were tested at all; and of all at school only about 5 per cent. were found to have received an education really worthy of the name, and such as they were likely to retain.

seed, as soon as it is sprouted, withers and dries up, and never grows into a crop for the feeding of the nation."* Looking, therefore, at all these things, is it not deliberate self-deception to hope that our primary schools can ever succeed in giving to the country anything in the remotest degree approaching to an educated electorate, unless the standard of instruction should be enormously raised, the whole class of teachers enormously improved, the period during which and the age up to which children remain at school greatly altered for the better, and provision made for their continuance under instruction in later life ? Who can expect that in a country so populous, so hard-working, and so hard-pressed as ours, children generally can be kept at school till the age of four- · teen ? And who can hope to make them qualified for the supreme political power we have conferred upon them unless they are? An educational franchise adopted years ago might have solved the problem, and given us what we want in time. But it is too late for that now.

A very plausible argument is, however, often urged against the validity of the above reasoning. "Granted," it is said, " that the education of the electoral masses not only is at present very defective, but in comparison with that of the ranks higher in the social scale must always remain so ;—granted that it can never become such as in any great degree really to qualify

---

* "The Struggle for National Education," by John Morley, *passim.* Reports of the Privy Council, 1873.

them to pronounce on general questions of policy, to decide the more difficult social and economic problems, or even to choose the best means to good ends ;—still it does not necessarily follow that they may not be fully qualified to exercise electoral functions, or that mischief will ensue in consequence of their being entrusted with electoral power in preponderating measure. What they have to determine at a general election is not this or that political or legislative proceeding, this or that social or economic principle or line of action, but which candidate on the whole they most esteem and can most confidently trust ; and a very moderate amount of education will enable them to do this. They have to judge men—not measures ; and for this mere ordinary sagacity and observation, mere native shrewdness, mere common sense in a word, is all that is required. Nay, more : it may even be argued that, in such numerous popular constituencies as ours, that sort of bucolic ignorance and conscious incapacity which will induce them and oblige them to trust blindly to their superiors in political matters will be far safer than such imperfect and superficial education as alone we can give them, and which would merely delude them into a pretension of judging for themselves. The old original conception of the electoral function was a selection of wise and good representatives, legislators, senators, rulers—not a *plebiscitum* on principles of policy or particular enactments; and the more we can return to that original conception the better. Let the people fix upon honest leaders, qualified candidates, men they know and can trust, in short, and all will be well. This, working-men electors can do readily enough without ever reaching the sixth standard, and even without remembering anything they learned at school."

Very well : there is much truth in these considerations, though I contest their relevancy here. I may, perhaps, request reference to a previous argument of mine (which for convenience of reference I reproduce as an Appendix),* where I pointed out as one of the great evils accompanying the Democratic form of Government, that large popular constituencies can never, or very seldom, think or decide for themselves in political matters, but will always as a fact get the thinking done for them, and the choice virtually taken out of their hands; that the more numerous the electoral body, the more wide and despotic will be the influence of wire-pullers and electioneerers ; and that democracies have a natural and irresistible tendency to become oligarchies—and oligarchies of the worst sort. But none the less is there an increasing tendency to make elections turn, not upon the choice of particular men, but upon the popularity of special measures. The thinking, it is true, is still done by the few for the many ; but the few labour to excite the many in behalf of their especial crotchets, and sometimes with ominous success ; so much so that we may live to see the House of Commons degenerate from an Assembly consisting of political *parties* divided

---

* Appendix A., "Mistake of Honest Democrats."

from each other by lines of general policy distinct in tone, if not in principle, into an assemblage of *cliques*, representing each an interest, a fanaticism, a social aim. The mischief has not yet gone deep, but the symptoms of it are plain enough to augur danger in the future. To say nothing of the uncomfortable electoral influence exercised by the Railway interest, and the Brewing or Publican interest, we have had electioneering wire-pullers of incredible dogmatism and activity insisting that no candidate shall be returned, whatever his political creed, who will not vote for the Permissive Bill; for the Repeal of the Contagious Diseases Act; for the Repeal of the Criminal Law Amendment Act, or the Masters' and Servants' Act, or the Mine Regulation Act; for Home Rule; for the Repeal of all Indirect Taxes; for the abolition of the great Direct Tax; for the establishment of Secular education, and so on :—all in turn endeavouring to hold the balance of parties, to force their own pet fanaticism or interest upon the country, and to make the election turn, not on the welfare of the Empire, but upon the success of their peculiar crotchet. Most of these men are honest, all of them are earnest, the aims of some of them are unquestionably important; but they are all men of *glimpses*, not men of *views*. They are fanatics, not statesmen, scarcely politicians; and all alike appeal to the ignorance and excitability of an untrained electorate on behalf of schemes and doctrines which would be laid before the sober sense of an educated electorate in vain. All alike—which is our present point—seek to make the election turn, not on the choice of competent men, but on preference for particular opinions or a special question. They alike insist on the constituency forming a judgment on a given topic, or accepting *their* judgment.

But, further, we entirely dispute the main position of our objectors—namely, that no education, nothing beyond average common sense—is necessary to qualify the mass of electors to follow good leaders and choose good representatives. Possibly, if they were let alone, ordinary sense and feeling might suffice. Possibly they would then choose, in preference to ranting demagogues, the landlords who had been considerate and beneficent, the employers who had been just and kindly, the candidates favoured by the clergyman who had tended them in sickness and comforted them in sorrow, the neighbour who had helped them in trouble or advised them when in perplexity, or whom they had known for years as a model of wise and steady philanthropy. But they never are let alone. There are always at hand, now that they have become a power in the State, agitators, demagogues, and leaders who desire to wield that power for their own purposes, and to indoctrinate the electors in their own views ; who persuade them (too truly, often) that they are ill-off, and (often very falsely) that they (these advisers) will make them better off ;—that their landlords are selfish and exact too high a rent ; that their employers are grasping and oppressive, and pay them too scanty wages ; that their clergyman is a deceiver,

in league with their superiors, who humbugs them
about a future world to keep them quiet in this, and
that their benevolent neighbours do not do half enough
for them, and so on. There may be truth enough in
these representations to hide from the ignorant hearers
the preponderance of falsehood they contain ; this at
all events is certain, that more than ordinary moral
training, besides some disciplined intelligence, is required to enable an elector to prefer the man who
preaches unwelcome wisdom to the man who tickles
his ears with alluring nonsense—the man who seeks
to moderate his hopes to the man who labours to
excite and flatter them—the man who endeavours to
instil content to the man who tries to stimulate ambition—the moralist who points to temperance and
thrift as the ways to competence, rather than the
orator who expatiates on the easier and more attractive
path of higher earnings and more liberal allowances.
It is so easy to deceive those who have never been
taught to reason, discriminate, or sift ; who do not
and cannot know, in five cases out of six, which of the
statements confidently told them are true and which
are false, nor which of the arguments are valid and
which are simply futile and shallow. We fully admit
that the result we foresee has not yet appeared in our
Parliamentary elections ; that few bad men have been
chosen, and that few fallacious or dangerous cries have
succeeded at the hustings. But this is partly because
the uneducated portion of the constituencies are as
yet in a minority on the register ; partly because so

large a portion of the working classes mistrust (and
rightly mistrust) their class leaders, and under the
ballot are beginning to give expression to that mistrust; partly, too, and largely, because the old habit
of deferring to their social superiors has not yet died
out.   But if we wish to realise to ourselves how easily
the working classes are misguided in their choice of
leaders, and how much harm they do suffer and might
inflict in consequence, we have only to study the
recent history of Trade Union action; bearing in
mind, as we study, that here—if ever—we are dealing with subjects which working men might be
expected to understand, and with leaders whom they
ought to be able to see through.

It may be worth while to notice here a slow and
subtle change in the class of members on whom the
choice of popular constituencies has a tendency to
fall, which dates probably from the first Reform Bill,
but which has become more marked with every fresh
extension of the franchise, and which bids fair to
influence the constitution and character of the House
of Commons in a direction little suspected at the outset.   It seems probable that some of our democratic
moves may produce effects the very reverse of democratic, opening wider and wider the doors of political
life to rank and wealth, especially to hereditary wealth,
and closing them more and more to real talent when
unsupported by these adventitious aids.   Previous to
1832 the chiefs of both the great parties in the State
watched eagerly for dawning genius at the Universities

and elsewhere, promptly encouraged and enlisted in the service of the State young men of promise and capacity, introduced them into Parliament by means of close boroughs, and thus gave them an opportunity at once of showing and of training their powers, as well as of learning betimes the business of administration. When once they had won their spurs in office or debate, and publicly justified the expectations formed of their ability, when once they became known to the electorate and to the world in general, it was comparatively easy for them to maintain their position as tried politicians, and to obtain seats for open and populous constituencies. *Now*, youthful ambition, if without wealth or high connection, finds no such opening to a coveted career. Counties and boroughs look out for tried and known candidates, and these poor men of capacity and promise cannot get a trial, and have no means of making themselves known. If they inherit great wealth, constituencies will often choose them for their fathers' sake ; if they are scions of noble families they can be brought forward and pushed on by the influence of their connections. Now, unendowed, impoverished, struggling ability is essentially democratic in its temper, and generally in its aims ;—yet it is precisely this unendowed ability which is being elbowed out of public life in England *in limine*, by the secondary and unanticipated operation of the lowering of the electoral franchise. But this is not all. There is an increasing tendency in the larger cities and the more populous boroughs *to* prefer candidates of local reputation, who have become favourites with their fellow-citizens either from the respect due to their character or for services rendered to the town. These are often men of wealth, of sense, of ability, and richly deserve the distinction awarded to them. But they are nearly always, by the necessity of the case, past middle life ;—they have *acquired* their local influence, not inherited it,—and influence of this sort is only acquired by the steady toil of years ;—they have been trained to business, not to politics or to administration, and it is too late for them, in the vast majority of cases, to go to school in a new profession. Moreover, they are as a rule, and almost *ex vi termini*, men of regular and quiet habits, and a change at the age of fifty and upwards from these habits to the late hours and exciting atmosphere of the House of Commons is fatal to them.* Occasionally, no doubt, a few men of this description, such as Mr Forster, Mr Stansfeld, and Mr W. H. Smith, gain their position while still in the prime of life, and not too stiff to work in official harness ; but these are exceptions, and political training is not easily begun even at the age when they entered the House of Commons. Mr Goschen sat for London while still a

---

* The majority of these men are Liberals, for usually the strength of the Liberal party lies in commercial and manufacturing constituencies. In the last session it is said the Liberals lost *thirty-nine* members by death, and the Conservatives only *sixteen*. The average age of the members for London, Manchester, Liverpool, Birmingham, Leeds, Bradford, Edinburgh, Bristol, and Sheffield, is at present *fifty-nine* years.

young man ; but his firm ranked very high among the merchants of the City for wealth and reputation, and the City is not precisely a popular constituency.

Now the effect of these several influences, it would appear, must almost certainly be in the end that, whatever section of the community preponderate at the poll, whoever may be "the governing classes," the actual members of the Government, the Parliamentary Rulers of the country, will become more and more the men of *inherited* rank or wealth, members in some sort of the aristocracy in short. It has not been so hitherto, I fully admit ; but the indications that it will be hereafter would appear to be unmistakable.*

Perhaps we may even go a step further, and predict that a larger proportion than hitherto of Ministers, especially of Cabinet ministers, will in future be Members of the Upper House. Already it is thought by some that the preponderance of political ability, of trained political ability at least, even of political wisdom and sagacity perhaps, lies with the House of Lords. The active Members of that House gain their education in the Commons ; they are constantly recruited from the Commons and often from the *élite* of the Commons; they start in public life with vast advantages, and they start as a rule much earlier. But whatever may be the case relatively, we should be disposed to predict that in time, and no

---

* The new House of Commons contains 149 Members belonging to or immediately connected with the aristocracy, and we believe more millionaires or sons of millionaires than any preceding House.

long time, the positive average capacity, the average
political experience of the Upper House will increase
while that of the Lower House will decline.
Probably even the average age of the Commons will
increase till it passes that of the Lords—of the
Senators par excellence.* In any case the practical
working rulers and administrators of the country will
be chosen more and more from those who begin their
public life from a vantage ground—from the aristocracy or the plutocracy in short. It is impossible that
a combination of influences such as these should not
largely modify the operation of our political system,
and perhaps even go some way to counteract the
menacing dangers which it is the object of this Paper
to point out.

Many, I am aware,—especially "rurals," who take
their ideas from the mental atmosphere that prevails
about their ordinary residences—are inclined to make
light of all timid or gloomy auguries, trusting to the
power of Property, and the respect that hitherto has
always been paid to men of property in England. No
doubt the strength derived from vast possessions is
still great in this country. It is upheld partly by

---

* It is the impression of experienced eyes that the present
House looks decidedly younger than its predecessor ; which, as it
may be regarded as a *reactionary* House, is a confirmation of this
notion. The actual figures bearing on this subject are as follows :—

Average age of present House of Commons . 48½ years.
    ,,   ,,   late   ,,   ,,   . 50½ ,,
    ,,   ,,   House of Lords in 1874 . . 54½ ,,

mere snobbism, partly by a well-grounded conviction that, somehow, wealth has extraordinary facilities in general for obtaining what it wishes, which poverty has not, partly from undefined but still very influential sentiments which have descended to us from the feudal times. Property, it is fancied, in the future as in the past, will overawe voters and will guide, or command votes. As long as property is safe from attack, political power in the hands of poverty, it is thought, need not be feared.—I believe this to be a perilous delusion, though, looking merely at the outside and surface of affairs, I am not surprised at its being so confidently entertained. No doubt the sacredness of the rights of property is still one of the strongest sentiments of Englishmen. No doubt property has still vast influence, regular and irregular, legitimate and illegitimate, direct and circuitous, over those who have it not. No doubt any distinct and straightforward attack upon the rights of property would be promptly and easily defeated; but rights may be undermined as well as assaulted in front, and there is sure to be much sapping of foundations before any face attack is ventured on. In a fair fight, unquestionably, the Propertied Classes *versus* the Proletariat would have a quick victory now:—they will even have an easy victory, if they open their eyes and close their ranks in time. But will they do this, and are they doing it? The sapping and mining process has been already commenced, in practice as well as in theoretical teaching, and the full scope of neither has yet been fully comprehended. This theoretical teaching may not be unsound, and it certainly is plausible ; the practical action as yet may have done no harm. But the work is begun : the influence is in operation. Railways have established the doctrine that a man's property, especially landed property, may be forcibly taken from him for public objects, or for what pushing and energetic men can plausibly represent as such. Exemption of small incomes is the thin end of the wedge—the line by which a graduated income-tax is first approached. The clamour, supported by many financiers and by some arguments not wholly bad, for abolishing indirect taxation, and virtually placing all fiscal burdens upon realised property, is another ominous indication. The claims put forward by J. S. Mill, for the confiscation of the "unearned increment" of land to the coffers of the State, is a movement in the same direction more serious still. The entirely new and very decided provisions of the Irish Land Bill (their justice or wisdom I do not now discuss) gave up the entire *principle* of the sacredness of property, and may be said to have conceded and canonised the doctrine (possibly a true one) that *all* property may be confiscated, if only a strong case, or an equally strong case, can be made out in favour of the scheme. Yet all these things were done in the green tree, before Household Suffrage was enthroned, or at least before it had fairly grasped its sceptre. But why dwell on these things ? Why do we always forget that, *potentially* if not actually, the power of Property, the rights of property, the sacredness of property, have been signed away already? Do not the Poor Laws virtually *give to the Poor* a first mortgage on all the property of the Rich?* And how will it fare with us when the masses—preponderating at the poll, selecting the House of Commons, swaying the Lawyers, dictating the laws, nominating our rulers—shall be in a position to determine how the . Poor Laws shall be administered?

All these are extreme results, it will be said, wholly speculative, monstrous and impossible. I admit that they are extreme, but they are logical. They are improbable, but by no means impossible. I do not anticipate their realisation ; on the contrary, I feel sanguine hope that they will be averted. But I am sure of this, that logical consequences from causes already put in action will be realised, and will not be averted, unless some modifying and counteracting agencies of adequate cogency are brought to bear, and brought to bear in time.

I seem to see the quarter whence salvation from the dangers I have indicated is to come—if it come at all. It is not difficult to point out the counteracting influences and agencies to which we must appeal :—it may be very difficult to get those agencies to work, and to work with sufficient energy, and .to work widely enough, and to work before it is too late. The power of the masses and their preponderance on

---

* The destitute, or semi-destitute, poor at least.

the electoral register are augmenting annually and
rapidly ; the social and moral changes to which we
have to trust to make them exercise that preponderant power for the public good, march at a fearfully
slow pace in comparison. The inertia of all existing
things is incalculable. Still this inertia, if a difficulty,
is also a source of safety. If the masses are slow to
be elevated, institutions are also slow to be upset or
undermined. The late general election, not only in
its main results, but in some of its detailed features,
is full of hope and promise. It has shown that the
country is still sound at heart ; that the *instincts* of
the people—however inarticulate their utterances,
however confused their reasoning, however mixed
their elements—are on the whole healthy. It has, by
inaugurating (for it inaugurated rather than established)
the operation of the ballot, broken the neck of two
tyrannies, far more onerous and mischievous than the
special tyranny against which it was originally directed
—the tyranny of Party and the tyranny of Trades
Unions. Men have been able to give expression to
their honest feelings and convictions without dread of
being reproached by their associates or punished by
their fellow workmen. Unskilled labourers, who are
a large majority, have caught a welcome glimpse of
possible emancipation from the cruel oppression of
skilled and organised minorities, who, at their caprice,
or for their imagined interests, so often deprived them
of employment, but rarely contributed to their maintenance. More than all, by canvassing, public meet-

ings, and electioneering gatherings, the election has
advanced the political education of the constituencies
to a degree which those best qualified to judge declare
is most encouraging, and which seems to indicate that,
if candidates and members do their duty with courage
and capacity, a vast amount of enlightenment and instruction may be disseminated even among those who
have never known the benefits of school.

For the future, our main security will be in *the
wider diffusion of Property*, and in all such measures
as will facilitate this result. With the possession of
property will come Conservative instincts and disinclination for rash and reckless schemes. It is not in
itself a political education, but it forms an excellent
basis for it. Peasant-Proprietorship, held out as an
economic panacea, appears to me (as I have elsewhere
argued at length*) to involve a distinct fallacy. But
where it arises naturally, and not as an artificial product of legislation directed to a special end, it may be,
and usually will be, a political and social influence for
good. We trust much, therefore, to the rural popula-
lation becoming Proprietors, and to the urban population becoming Capitalists. And it is to be hoped that
the two processes may go on *pari passu*, so as to
avoid the mischief so salient in France—severance and
class hostility, as well as utter discrepancy of ideas
and temperaments, between town and country, between citizens and cultivators. Now, is this process

---

* " Essays on Political and Social Science—' Laing's Peasant
Proprietorship.' "

(the acquisition of property by our labouring classes) going on ? What are its prospects ? And how best can it be hastened and secured ? It will be seen that the outlook, though not exactly bright, can scarcely be considered as discouraging.* We give here the merest summary of the facts, the details of which may be sought in the writings referred to below.

The agricultural population present obviously the greatest difficulty. For them to become proprietors without the assistance, without indeed the continued countenance and forbearance, of landowners, would seem nearly impossible. They are scattered, and cannot readily combine, like town artizans, for any purpose that requires the co-operation of numbers to work it out. They are sparsely strewed over the country ; they must live near their work, mostly on their employers' farms, and therefore cannot readily profit by building societies or similar institutions. They cannot (even if they have saved the means) buy land in small lots, surrounding or adjacent to their own cottages, unless their masters or the large proprietors in the neighbourhood are willing, as a kindness and with the patriotic view of raising their labourers in the social scale, to sell them such small lots out of their

---

* Fuller elucidation of the subject may be found in the *Quarterly Review*, No. 263 : " Proletariat on a Wrong Scent."—*Edinburgh Review*, No. 281 : "Savings of the People."—*Fortnightly Review*, Feb. 1874 : " Prospects of Co-operation," by Henry Fawcett.—" Political Problems," by W. R. Greg.—" Trade Unions and Partnerships," p. 132.—"Agricultural Labour," by Sir Baldwin Leighton, Bart.

own estate. Nor unfortunately is there any security that, if every cottager had given to him, or had purchased, an acre or a couple of acres near his own dwelling, he would retain it for a single generation, or for moré than a few years, unless prevented from selling it by law or by contract; for, land being limited and greatly coveted, rich men will always be found ready to offer him twice or ten times its actual *value* for his small possession.* · But there is no reason why wealthy and enlightened landowners should not do this great thing for the peasants on their property; nor why others, less rich and enlightened now, should not ere long follow their example; still less, why adequate allotments should not be awarded to every

---

* When you have given the peasant his acre, or his five acres, or his ten, *how are you to secure that he shall retain it?* Short of a jubilee year like that which the Israelitish legislator is said to have enacted—short of declaring this peasant's farm inalienable, sacred from any claim, untouchable for any debt, unforfeitable for any negligence, misuse, or drunken incapacity, indivisible among any heirs—how is he to keep it? We once had a race of small proprietors (yeomen) in certain counties of England. They have all died out, drunk themselves out, been bought out. When common lands have been inclosed, what has always become of the few acres allotted in actual property to the commoners adjoining? In every case they have been sold to tempting bidders or forfeited for debts. Why shut our eyes to the fact that in densely-peopled countries land (like jewels) becomes a luxury only attainable to, or retainable by, the rich; it can only be purchased or possessed by those who have spare means, and *can afford themselves a superfluity.* The rich man can afford to be satisfied with 2 per cent. for his money (and land rarely yields more); the poor man must have 5 or 10 per cent. The peasant has inherited a farm worth £100 in fee simple, or he has given £100 for it, or a land society has enabled

cottage, on the careful and judicious plan expounded
in Sir Baldwin Leighton's pamphlet, and tested by his
experience; nor why other benevolent and sagacious
gentlemen should not try the scheme essayed by Mr
Brand (the Speaker of the House of Commons), of
making his labourers virtually partners in the profits
of his farm; nor why the analogous experiments,* at
Assington and elsewhere, of co-operative farming
should not be introduced on a more extensive scale.
Since it is certain that a County Household Suffrage
will shortly make the majority of peasants voters, and
since the ballot will make them independent voters, it
is plainly the interest of every landlord, as of every
farmer, to raise and educate his labourers as well as

---

him to pay £100 by difficult instalments. He is proud of it, and
attached to it. But a neighbouring proprietor, or a retired tradesman who wants a villa and a garden, offers him £250, £350, £500
for it—is he likely to refuse the offer? Ought he to refuse? Men
will always be at hand to give him for his acres more than they
are worth: they want them for pleasure, not for profit. They
desire them, as they desire jewels, for fashion, for beauty, not
caring the least for the return they yield. Five hundred pounds
an acre to the millionaire is nothing—to the peasant owner, it is
wealth. Therefore, we say that, create as many peasant properties as you please, they will all be swallowed up in a few years by
the natural process of sale—unless either peasants become fewer
and better paid, and possessed therefore of a superfluity, able to
afford themselves a luxury, and *an ostensibly bad or inferior invest-
ment*—or unless you actually forbid the sale of such properties :—
that is, add a new and more stringent restriction to those which
these very enthusiasts are seeking to remove—tie up land in a
stricter settlement than any of those against which their clamour
is just now so righteously directed.

   * Sir Baldwin Leighton, p. 15.

to conciliate and attach them. Small allotments, small properties even, would not render the men independent of wages; while most assuredly they would render their feelings more friendly, and in time also their labour more intelligent and therefore more efficient. And the comfort of a labourer's position can be so largely affected by the goodwill of his employer in a score of ways, that wide-spread alienation or marked success of Union leaders could scarcely exist in any district where every peasant has fair wages and his acre or half-acre of land, either in occupation or in fee. We have no more doubt that it would be a wise benevolence on the part of landowners to secure this advantage to every cottager on their estate, than we have that these cottagers, without such sagacious and kindly aid, can never secure it for themselves. But on the whole there is a good deal to warrant hopes of a great improvement in the agricultural labourer's * position; migration and emigration are fast becoming familiar ideas to him, and wages are irresistibly rising in consequence; frugality in the expenditure of those earnings he has already learned; and a vote, with the shield of the ballot, will make it the interest of his employer and his landlord to befriend him.

As regards the skilled or half-skilled artizans, the case is far clearer. The acquisition of property, the accumulation of capital, is already in their power, and legislation has but few further facilities to give or

---

* Sir Baldwin Leighton, p. 15.

obstacles to remove. Their earnings are now so
large that only soberer habits and sounder sense are
needed to make them independent capitalists in less
than half a lifetime. The following passage places
the matter in a clear light.

"Among the colliers of South Wales, for example, a
man can earn 6s., and even 8s. a day, and even more in
special cases. The family income, therefore, cannot be
estimated at less than £3 a week, or say, £150 per annum.
If it were not for the exhausting, unnecessary, and (as will
presently be seen) noxious drafts made upon the means of
these people by the Union funds—perhaps even *with* this
drawback,—a man might easily lay by £50 a year, and live
in comfort on the remainder. A skilled operative in various
branches of the iron trade can earn also £3 a week, with
the aid of an assistant (often his own son), to whom he
pays 10s. or 15s. In the cotton trade, the more skilful
and industrious hands can often earn 30s. or 40s. a week ;
and, as three or four of a family are often employed, their
aggregate income often reaches 50s. or 60s. or more. And
so on. Now in all these cases—and, though we do not
say they are *average* specimens, they are assuredly very
frequent and widely attainable ones—the workman might
in ten years have £500 in the bank ; and twenty such
men, combining their savings, would be able to commence
business or to join other industrials with a capital of
£10,000, and a credit, owing to their character and their
funds, which would readily command £5000 more at least.
It is, therefore, obviously in the power of industrious,
steady, skilful, and frugal workmen to become capitalists
before middle age ; and it is their own fault if they do not.

"So much for direct proof. Now for still more irrefragable and convincing circumstantial evidence. We have seen what operatives might save. We will now show what they do waste. The annual expenditure of the population of the United Kingdom in fermented liquors and tobacco exceeds £100,000,000 ; that in beer and spirits only reaches £75,000,000. In England alone, the consumption of intoxicating liquors would allow an expenditure of £10, 15s. 6d. to each adult male. Now, according to the best estimates that can be formed, the expenditure of the working classes alone in drinking and smoking is not far from £60,000,000—of which £40,000,000 is mere extravagance and excess. Every year, therefore, the working classes have it in their power to become capitalists (*simply by saving wasteful and pernicious expenditure*) to an extent which would enable them to start at least 500 cotton mills, or coal mines, or iron works, *on their own account*, or to purchase at least 500,000 acres, and so set up 50,000 families each with a nice little estate of their own of ten acres, in fee simple. No one can dispute the facts. No one can deny the inference. After this, what must we think of the sense or honesty or morality of the Proletaires who wish to confiscate the land or the capital of others, or of the leaders who would persuade them it would be right and wise to do so ? Were we not warranted in saying that the fate and future of the working classes, their salvation or their ruin, lie in their own hands,—and in no others?"— *Proletariat on a False Scent.*

This shows what might be done. The papers to which we have referred give us some indication of what has been done. Already the savings of the operatives, invested in Building societies, Friendly societies, Co-operative stores and industries, amount to many millions, besides the accumulations in Savings' banks.* The Quarterly Reviewer shows that, under the present condition of the retail trade, the working classes as a rule pay at least 10 per cent. more for the articles they consume than they would do under a sounder system ; and Professor Fawcett gives excellent reasons for estimating this loss at nearer 20 per cent. Messrs Chambers (than whom there are few higher authorities in these matters) estimate what they call the mis-expenditure of the working classes at a total of upwards of *one-third* of their income, or not less than a *hundred millions* annually.† If then, taking the data furnished by the sources already referred to, we add together the sums which the working classes actually do save, the sums which they waste in noxious or excessive indulgences, the sums lost by unskilful purchasing and house-keeping, and in unsafe and unprofitable investments, their power under wiser auspices of becoming capital-ists cannot be gainsaid. And Capitalists and Pro-prietors may not always be sagacious or generous politicians, but they are usually Conservative, and never revolutionary.

---

* *Savings' Banks* £60,000,000, much in the hands of working men ; *how* much we do not know. *Co-operative undertakings,* capital invested £7,000,000. *Friendly Societies* estimated at £15,000,000. *Building Societies,* large sums, but amount un-known.

† The author of "The Proletariat on a False Scent," brings out an almost exactly similar result.

When all is said, however, when every due allowance has been made for counteracting and mitigating
influences, the chief fact is still undisputed and the
chief peril remains to be confronted. The State may
do its little all to discourage drinking, to facilitate
good investments and discountenance deceptive ones;
schools will do something, and election speeches and
penny newspapers will do much to enlighten the ever
extending and renewed Constituencies;—the more
general acquisition of property will in time diffuse its
far more effectual teachings;—experience will instruct
and disappointment will warn many;—and wise and
just legislation and administration, it may be hoped,
will emancipate the unskilled labourer from the cruel
oppression of his skilled brethren. But these saving
processes of elevation and moralisation are inevitably
slow, while the multiplication of men is alarmingly
rapid, and that of voters more rapid still; and, (what
must never be forgotten) the multiplication of the
poorer and less educated voters far more rapid than
that of the more trained and qualified. It is true
that the *personnel* of Parliament may be little
changed; few illiterate candidates or mere artizans
may find their way into the House of Commons, and
the rich and noble may in future preponderate there
as much as ever; the new and altered Constituencies
may not *discard* their old representatives, but they
will *demoralise* them—far the worst evil of the two
—by lowering the tone, contracting the scope, and
warping and diverting the objects of their policy.

For assuredly, if you fancy that you can lower the average intelligence of an electoral body without lowering the average wisdom and character of the representatives that body will return, you are dreaming that foolishest of all dreams—that you can establish a cause and yet escape the consequence. And that an electoral body in which the uneducated largely, unavoidably, and increasingly outnumber the educated —and in which the more refined, thinking, and timid of that educated minority retire from the conflict in which they feel themselves habitually overpowered, as its terms grow harder, its warfare rougher, and its rewards more scanty—that such a set of constituencies (as compared with constituencies of selecter elements) *must* decline in intelligence and tone and range of view, though possibly not in selfishness of aim, would seem to be absolutely certain.* Let us not be deceived or lulled to sleep—encouraged we may well be—by the unexpected issue of the late election. A number of causes contributed to that result, which can scarcely operate again—not, at least, in combination. The wage-receiving classes had not yet established their numerical majority on the register; the growing uneasiness of the propertied classes at the vaguely-menacing prospect before them had become almost alarm ;

---

* France, Switzerland, and Belgium afford us experimental confirmation, and the United States more significantly still. See especially a paper published in the *National Review*, April 1861, entitled, "Three Men and Three Eras," reproduced with a copious supplement as Appendix C.

the ballot enabled every one—the labourer oppressed by Trades' Unions, and the liberal indignant at the radicalism towards which he felt he was being dragged —for the first time to express his honest sentiments ; —disgust and scorn at the Home-Rule intrigue, which it was feared might become serious if a Liberal Government were in office, and in difficulties— touched a new chord of patriotism in Tory and in Whig alike ;—while the peculiarly rasping fashion in which the economising fanaticism of the Liberal Chiefs had been carried out by their subordinates had irritated every section of the Civil Service into not unnatural hostility and rage ; and, to crown the whole, the best friends of retrenchment had been alienated from a ministry which caricatured and discredited their doc-trines, and which could not perceive that " when tax-ation ceases to be oppressive, parsimony ceases to be popular." But a general election six years hence may give a very different answer to a ministerial appeal ;— unless, indeed, the interval be so employed by a sagaci-ous government as to satisfy the new constituent masses that their interests have formed its steady, resolute and earnest aim.

It will be objected that if the views promulgated in these pages be correct, the prospect before the civil-ized world is the reverse of cheerful. If the progress of democracy do indeed logically lead to the conclu-sions I have pointed out, if the practice of handing over political power and the command of legislation increasingly to the less enlightened classes must operate to render Government and laws less sagacious and beneficent,—then, since the tendency of circumstances is decidedly set in this direction in nearly every country both in Europe and America, we can foresee little in the future but progressive decadence in all the higher elements of national life.—I cannot gainsay the inference. I cannot see that the advances of democracy during the last fifty or seventy years in France, Spain, Switzerland, Belgium, the United States, and elsewhere, have offered results which invalidate the argument; I cannot at present discern the quarter from which reaction or rescue is to come, or the *Deus ex machinâ* who is to intervene ; and there is more faith than philosophy in our vague trust that harvest will not follow seed-time, and that causes, which in all previous history have been relentlessly fertile, will hereafter become preternaturally barren. It may be that the education of schools, the education of life, the education of penalty and failure, may in time so tell upon the minds of the less competent and less instructed classes as to induce them voluntarily to divest themselves of functions which others are more fitted to discharge. But of the dawn of that better day no preluding ray, however faint, is as yet visible in the clouded sky; and if it should come—as I with others hope in trembling—neither writer nor reader will survive to share its sunshine ; it will come in the fulness of time, when all of us shall be mute, and most of us forgotten.

This at least seems certain, if either our practical

instincts or our historical experience are to be trusted, that no political system can promise tranquillity or permanence which does not vest the constitutional supremacy in the same hands which already possess the actual preponderance. Now, this natural and actual preponderance—this *major vis* in ultimate resort—never lies with mere numbers; but always with rank, intellect, and wealth. These are the appanage of the comparatively few; and can only be prevented from remaining such by the most artificial and stringent restrictions alike upon the acquisition of property, its retention, and its testamentary disposition. Social superiority and electoral supremacy, if divorced from one another, must be ever in a state of conflict. Preponderance by legal right, and preponderance by actual fact, must lie with the same class if we are to have either peace or progress. If they do not, then *either* Property will wrest the voting power from the Proletariat, or dictate the use to be made of it; *or* the Proletariat will wrest property from the wealthy, or restrain its accumulation, or direct its division. Political power lies naturally with Intellect and Property, and what God·has joined man cannot put asunder with impunity.

II.

ECONOMIC ROCK.

THE second "Rock Ahead" I have named "The Approaching Industrial Exhaustion or Decline of Great Britain." To the popular mind the very phrase will sound absurd, and the notion it conveys will be dismissed as a groundless delusion. Not so to the more observant and the better informed of those energetic and enterprising "Captains of Industry" who have made Great Britain supreme among the productive nations of the earth. Their trained and vigilant eyes can already detect symptoms hidden from the inexperienced and unlearned; their keener ears already hear far-off sounds and murmurs ominous of the rising but still distant storm. The indications are not salient enough, nor the sounds loud enough as yet to force themselves on common observation; but those who do see and hear them well know that there can be no mistake as to their meaning or their menace. England has for generations been the great manufacturing country of Europe, far ahead of all others, the workshop of the world; it is difficult to believe that she can ever lose this supremacy. She is still far in advance of all rivals: why should we prognosticate the loss of her supremacy? Her industrial enterprise and wealth have in the most recent years been increasing at a rate unexampled in the past: why trouble ourselves to ask whether this increase has been relative or merely absolute? Why torment ourselves with dark forebodings about the *causes* of decline which you tell us are inaugurated and have begun to operate, when proofs and samples of the very reverse of decline stare us in the face on every side?—Such are the plausible representations against which Cassandra raises her warning voice in vain. She fully admits that the evils she foresees are as yet non-existent; that some of them may be avertible, and that all are possibly very distant:—she only argues that when once the seed is sown the harvest may be confidently looked for, though scarcely a blade of wheat or tares yet appears above the ground.

What are the qualities and advantages that have given us our manufacturing supremacy; that have enabled us to produce what every country in the world wants, better and cheaper and more abundantly than any other country? Mainly three :—

1. Abundant coal and iron, both cheap and in proximity.
2. The indefatigable industry and *workmanship* —by which I mean the blended skill and conscientiousness—of our artizans.
3. Our enormous command of capital.

Now, in all these points we are losing our *relative*, and in some our *positive* supremacy. Our coal is in process of exhaustion; it is daily and by a natural process becoming less abundant, and in consequence less cheap—and iron inevitably follows suit; our artizans work shorter hours, less steadily, and less conscientiously than formerly, while the skilled labour and enterprise of other nations are improving; and though our capital is more enormous than ever, it is increasingly at the command of foreign countries, which even in its acquisition are treading on our heels. From a combination of these causes the *cost of production* of the articles we manufacture and export is increasing, both positively and in comparison with competing countries. And this is true notwithstanding the astonishing expansion and elasticity of our foreign trade during the last decade*—an expansion which shows, not that the causes I signalise are not in operation, but simply that their operation has not yet become apparent; their effect being as yet only inchoate, or concealed by the counteraction of other agencies. I will abstain from overloading my pages with statistics. The figures needed for the argument are not voluminous; they are for the most part easily accessible, and in the moderate form in which I propose to state them, will scarcely be disputed.

I. *Exhaustion of Coal.* The aggregate quantity of coal existing in the globe, theoretically and strictly,

---

* Exports of British Produce.   Total Imports and Exports.
1861 . . £125,000,000   1861 . . £377,000,000
1870 . . 200,000,000   1870 . . 547,000,000

may be said to be unlimited. Besides our own calculated or ascertained supply, which is estimated at 146,000 millions of tons, Belgium and Westphalia have extensive coal basins ; China is reported to have a coal area of 400,000 square miles, the United States of 500,000 square miles, of which 200,000 are probably workable, and British North America about 8000 square miles. In addition to this incalculable quantity, the possible Indian supply is estimated at 16,000 millions of tons. How much of the coal thus indicated lies within reach (that is, can be brought to the surface at a cost which the inhabitants of the world will be able to pay) we have no means of accurately stating ; but it may be assumed to be practically ample to set at rest all anxiety as to the future fuel of the human race. But to us, and for our immediate purpose, these figures and speculations are utterly irrelevant. Coal is too bulky an article to pay the cost of distant carriage by land or sea ; and if ever England is reduced to import her fuel from America or China, the day of her manufacturing prosperity—to say nothing of her supremacy, the matter now in question—will have set for ever.* The only practical subject for consideration is the amount and availability of our home supply.

This also, strictly speaking and theoretically, may be said to be ample, if not virtually boundless. Our present consumption is about 120 millions of tons

---

* See " The Coal Question," by W. S. Jevons, ch. xii.

yearly, or, throwing out the quantity exported, 108 millions; and at this rate the total estimated reserve existing would last above 1200 years. But, as will be seen, this calculation is subject to so many deductions, as to be not only unreliable, but purely deceptive.

1. The quantity existing in *known* coal-fields is not 146,000 millions of tons, but only 90,000 millions of tons.

2. Even this certain 90,000 millions includes all that exists down to a depth of 4000 feet; and it is not proved, but only hoped, that we can, as a rule, work shafts deeper than 3000 feet.

3. It is obvious that, unless some great check should come to our prosperity, and to our increasing population and manufacturing productiveness, our annual consumption of coal will go on augmenting, and will soon reach, not 120 millions of tons yearly, but twice, thrice, or four times that amount; in which case, as shown in the Report of the Royal Commission, the available coal-fields of Great Britain would be worked out, not in 1200 years, or in 1000 years, but in 636, or in 360, or even in 100.

4. But these figures only represent about half the facts wherein our danger lies. The essential question is not "how soon will our coal be worked out?" but "how soon will our *cheap* coal be worked out?" Though it may be perfectly possible, as far as physical and mechanical obstacles merely are concerned, to raise coal from a depth of 3000 or 4000 feet, it may be too expensive to make it worth while to raise it.

The real question is, not how much we *can* raise, but how much *it will pay* to raise. The cost of working increases, *ceteris paribus*, as the shafts go deeper. In fact, apart from economical contrivances and new inventions, what we may term the natural price of coal—*i.e.*, the cost of producing it—must augment year by year; the more so as we are now working our richest and most easily accessible veins, and are getting through them fast.*

The last paragraph contains the essence of the whole question; and it is upon this that I desire to concentrate public attention. What we need for the continuance of our manufacturing prosperity and the retention of our manufacturing supremacy *is not coal, but* CHEAP *coal.* If we cannot obtain coal at such prices as will enable us to produce iron, and cotton, woollen, flax, and silk goods more cheaply than other countries, or at least as cheaply, it is of no use to know that coal in inexhaustible abundance lies beneath our soil. Last year gave us a startling and much needed warning. The extent and suddenness of the advance may have been the result of combined panic and speculation; but much of it was warranted, and, in spite of dull and interrupted trade, a considerable proportion has remained. The average price of coal rose 10s. a ton; the consumers, whether householders, manufacturers, or railway companies, paid (to some-

---

* If our readers are disinclined to wade through the voluminous Blue books of the Royal Commission, they will find an excellent summary of facts in the *Edinburgh Review* for April 1873.

body, whether colliers, coal owners, carriers, or dealers, is of little consequence) £60,000,000 more than usual. Under an increased burden of this kind no industry could long be expected to thrive. Iron-masters, indeed, were able to raise their prices in proportion, and made vast profits; but in consequence the demand has fallen off, and the reaction has become very serious. Cotton manufacturers and others could not do so, and in many instances their increased expenditure in coal more than swept away all their gains. It is not too much to say that if coal had remained, and were to remain in future, at the highest rates of last year, a period of adversity would set in for the productive industry of Great Britain which in all likelihood would be permanent.* The prices of the products of that industry could not be proportionally raised without checking the demand, nor without enabling rival nations to supply a larger and larger portion of that demand. The manufactures of England would in the first instance cease to expand, as they have done for long years and generations, and then, as foreign competition filled the gap, begin to decline. *Cheap* Coal,

---

* Yet, be it remembered, as a most important portion of the argument, that while the high prices of 1873 were incompatible with the continued profitableness of our manufactures, *the low prices which prevailed for some years previously* (and, favoured by which, those manufactures had taken such vast expansion) *were insufficient to afford a reasonable profit to the coal-owners, or an adequate scale of wages to the men*, and could not therefore have been permanent. See Report of Coal Committee of the House of Commons of 1873. See also " Wages in 1873," by Mr Brassey, p. 12.

E

we repeat, is obviously and notoriously indispensable
to the continuance of our marvellous productiveness;
and how is cheap coal to be secured, when every
year we have to dive for it deeper and deeper into
the bowels of the earth, and to pay higher and higher
wages to the miners who produce it?

The case, broadly stated, lies in a nutshell, and
appears to present a dilemma from which there is no
escape. If (from the several agencies to which I shall
presently allude) coal should fall to and remain at or
near its former moderate price, and if in consequence
our manufactures (and, as a natural result, our population) should continue to flourish and expand at their
recent rate, then our *available* coal-fields will be exhausted in, say, *twelve* generations, and our *cheap* coal
in less—possibly much less—than *six*. A collapse,
perhaps ruinously sudden, will then inevitably overtake
us, and will affect a population not of 30,000,000 (as
now), but of 60,000,000.

If, on the contrary, the price of this article, so indispensable to all our productive industry, should remain
at the rates of last year, or should even continue to
advance (as, barring the agencies I am about to specify,
it cannot fail to do), then our manufactures, whether
textile or metallic, will have to bear an ever-increasing
burden, which will year by year augment their cost of
production, positively and relatively;* and which

---

* Thus, as a concrete illustration, the high prices of coal last
year increased the cost of making certain classes of cotton goods
three-eighths of a penny per pound. Now one penny per pound
is a full average rate of profit.

must therefore curtail the demand for them, and limit the numbers engaged in them, and the population which our country can support in comfort.—In a word, cheap coal is necessary to the prosperity of England as a manufacturing workshop—yet that very prosperity is distinctly antagonistic to cheap coal, and will preclude much hope of it. The agencies I am now about briefly to specify *may* indefinitely postpone the evil day, but seemingly cannot by any possibility avert it.

These agencies are three in number. Any one of them, or all together, will assuredly largely reduce the price of coal or curb its advance ; *but, unfortunately, high prices of coal would appear to be needed to put any one of them into efficient operation.* It is only prices continuously high that enforce those continuous economies and inventions that check high prices.

First. The waste in the extraction of coal, though in many districts largely reduced of late years, is still enormous. The *avoidable* waste is stated to vary from ten to thirty or forty per cent. But to limit this, as it ought to be and might be limited, would probably require to have the working colliers under better control than they are at present, or promise to become.

Secondly. Coal-cutting machines and other analogous appliances, if generally introduced, would economise the cost of extraction to an extraordinary extent —to what extent precisely we cannot say. Sanguine persons calculate that of 300,000 colliers now employed, two thirds might be dispensed with. Of course, such a sweeping economy would be vehemently opposed by the working-men concerned; but the obstacles thus presented, however serious, the law vigorously administered ought to be competent to overcome.

Thirdly. Economy in the consumption of coal, though considerable progress has already been made, offers an enormous margin still. It is calculated that about one-third of the coal consumed is used for Household purposes,* one-third for Steam-Engines, and one-third for Iron-making and other manufacturing processes. " In the first two divisions," says Sir William Armstrong, " the waste is simply shameful. . . . †

" In metallurgical and other manufacturing processes there is also room for much saving of coal ; but I must not extend my observations into that division of the subject. Speaking generally of coal consumption in all its branches, there can be little doubt that without carrying economy to its extreme limits, *all the effects we now realise from coal could be attained with half the quantity we use.* If a reduction to that, or any approximate extent, were effected, we should hear nothing more of scarcity or prohibitive prices for many years to come."

In short, there can be no question that it is within

---

* Against the undoubtedly very great margin for economy in the consumption of Household Coal is to be set (we must remember) the inevitable increase in that consumption for our increasing population.

† "The Coal Supply: Presidential Address," 1873. See also Siemen's calculations, and "The Coal Question," by W. S. Jevons. "Wages in 1873." Address by Mr Brassey.

our power so to economise the use of fuel as to lower the price to a very moderate figure ; but whether that figure would allow ample wages to men, or adequate profits to masters, is by no means clear. Moreover, the first effect of such reduced price would probably be to give a vast stimulus to consumption, and to discourage those very saving habits and processes which had produced the reduction. Still, economical contrivances, once introduced, would in general be retained, and at all events some thousands of millions of tons would have been reserved, and many additional years of prosperity secured to our manufacturers. Again, however, the evil day would only have been postponed : — the fact would still remain that we are incessantly drawing on an exhaustible supply, and a supply which, year by year, or generation by generation, *must* grow more costly.*

, II. *Deterioration in the Character of British Labour.* By "character" we mean efficiency and conscientiousness. Here again the causes are in operation, but the effects are only beginning to be obvious ; and as there is much to screen or confuse them, it is our habit to doubt or disbelieve them. English labour used, beyond that of every other

---

* Mr Brassey states that colliery wages rose between 1869 and 1873 upwards of 75 per cent., or from 21s. to nearly 37s. a week ; while, according to Mr Pease and Mr Macdonald, *the cost of raising coal* in Northumberland had increased from 60 to 65 per cent.— " Wages in 1873," p. 11.

nation, to be dogged, untiring, thorough, and honest. Its *quality* could be relied upon, and its willing, persevering energy was unrivalled. English workmen were never very sober, and therefore by no means exactly to be called steady ; but they were manageable by their employers, and exceptionally intelligent ; they were not given, like so many continental labourers, to holiday-making or pleasure-seeking ; when they did work, they worked with a will ; they neither shirked their task nor scamped it. If half we hear, and much we see, be true, this can scarcely be said now, as a rule, of any class of British labourers except navvies. In many departments of industry, we are assured, the chief aim of the operatives and the distinct purpose of their trade regulations, is to work as short hours as they can, and do as little in those hours as they can contrive in return for the wages they receive. Probably the statement is exaggerated or coloured ; but no one can say that it is groundless.

As to the hours of labour there can be no mistake. The matter is notorious and avowed. These hours in every trade are shorter than they used to be, and a concurrent agitation has been going on for years for a still further reduction. In factories they have been cut down from 12 to 10 (or rather from 72 hours a week to 54) ; and there is now a general demand for nine hours or for eight *per diem*. Even while we write Mr Mundella is bringing in a Nine Hours' Bill, and the Government has agreed to a most questionable and ominous compromise. We need waste no words as

to the fact :*—let us give a few minutes' consideration to its meaning. *Primâ facie* it would seem to
involve a diminished productiveness of labour by one-
tenth or one-fifth, and an augmented cost of production by something more. Let us see what modifications or deductions, if any, must be made before we
accept this conclusion in its entirety.

The sole point for controversy lies here :—Does a
reduction in the hours of labour from ten to eight
(say) involve, as a rule—*subject indeed to exceptions
and mitigations, but to none that invalidate the
conclusion*—a corresponding diminution in the produce of that labour ? " No," say theorists and some
practical men whose experience has been limited to
certain occupations and certain races—" men who are
fresh for eight hours' work are exhausted by ten ;
they can work so much harder for the shorter period
than for the longer, that they will turn out just as
much of any article, and get through just as big a
job."—In the case of actual manual labour, whether
the tool the man works with be a spade or a more
complicated or machine-like instrument, there is an
undoubted element of truth in the argument ; but,
when stated thus extravagantly, the truth is pushed

---

* A certain diminution of the hours of labour has been recently
effected by the " Mines Regulation Act," which has gone for
something in the increase of the price of coal ; but the artificial
limitation of hours by Union proceedings, and the general agitation in this direction among so many trades, are the features of
the time on which I wish to fix attention.

into a falsehood. To fancy that a man commencing his day's work measures his strength and proportions his energy according to the number of hours he knows that work is to last, will be pronounced absurd by the observation of every one who has superintended manual labourers. To assume that men's vigour is so impaired by ten hours' bodily exertion—that in practice *an equally well-fed labourer* who habitually works only eight hours will, in the course of the year and habitually, be one-fourth more vigorous and his labour one-fourth more efficient than his fellow who habitually works ten hours, is a plain fallacy or extravagance which no foreman of navvies or watcher of hedgers and ditchers paid by the piece will endorse. Practically, the assertion very nearly amounts to this self-contradictory and nonsensical assertion—that of two equally able-bodied and well-fed labourers, the one who lays down his spade and wheelbarrow at four o'clock will have done as much work as the one who toils on till six o'clock ; in fact, *that nothing at all is done in the last two hours.* The utmost that can be conceded is that in ordinary labour a man working for only eight hours instead of ten may turn out (say) eight and a half hours' work ; that an artizan on piece work, *determined to earn his usual wages, and not caring to earn more than those wages, or tied out by Trades Union regulations from doing so,* may earn that amount in eight hours nearly as well as in ten ; and that in the severer sorts of labour, such as coal-cutting, a maximum of eight hours may be the best for a man's permanent energy. The average is now greatly below this.

In the case of that enormous proportion of our industry, especially in the textile fabrics, where machinery is the producing agent, the real labourer, and the operative or artizan merely the vigilant attendant, the assertion we are combating is simply ludicrous. The machinery runs at the same speed whether it runs for eight hours or for ten, and produces almost exactly the same amount of fabrics *per hour;* and the utmost that can be alleged is that the quality of the product is liable to be sometimes and somewhat impaired where the attention of the watcher grows slack in consequence of too protracted hours. To avoid any charge of misstatement or over-statement, however, it must be admitted that some kinds of machinery (such as mules, looms, winding frames, &c.) are more dependent on the spinner and weaver for their continuous productiveness than others (such as throstles, carding-frames, &c.). In the former case some attendants may, no doubt, by greater energy and more unrelaxing vigilance, get as much out of their machines in (say) 54 hours as others will in 56 or 58. But the inference often so confidently drawn by superficial thinkers, or outsiders unacquainted with manufacturing towns from the fact that the reduction of factory hours from twelve to ten some years ago has not been attended with any diminution of the quantity of yarns or calicoes, or silk produced—is utterly irrelevant. The diminished productions which would inevitably

have resulted from the shorter hours has been
made good simply by more perfect machinery and
higher speed ; but this process of improved machinery
and augmented speed has always been going on, quite
independently of any consideration of established
hours ; and no one can doubt that if a given number
of improved looms and spindles produce as much yarn
and cloth in ten hours now as the old looms and
spindles did in twelve hours in 1834, they would
produce proportionally more in twelve hours now.

We are, therefore, justified in assuming—and shall
proceed to argue on the assumption—that (subject to
the very limited modification admitted in the case of
manual labour) a reduction of the hours of labour
means a corresponding (or nearly corresponding) reduction in the aggregate productiveness of that
labour.*

I am perfectly aware that some parties, among
whom is to be found the respected name of Mr Thomas
Brassey, persist in disputing this conclusion, but their
arguments seem to me never very close, and their illus-
trations are nearly always vitiated by some irrelevancy
or some want of parallelism in the facts adduced.†
Either they compare foreign labour with British ; or

---

* Mr Brassey mentions one trade where the diminution in the
work turned out was *far more* than proportioned to the reduction
in the hours of work.—" Wages in 1873," p. 30.

† The reply to these reasoners which appeared in *Fraser's Magazine* in Sept. 1872, may be quoted here: " For what does the
'nine-hours movement,' fairly and systematically carried out,
involve and mean? It means simply a reduction *pro tanto* (or

a well-fed with an underfed labourer ; or an artizan on
piece-work with one on day wages ; or operatives tending perfect with operatives tending inferior machines ;

---

within a very small fraction) of the productiveness of all labour, and
a corresponding increase in the price of all commodities. For do
not let us delude ourselves, as some are trying to do, into the
belief that as much—or anything near as much—can or will be
produced in nine hours as now in ten. To fancy this is to imply,
in the case of all textile industries at least, that it is the tenter of
the machine, and not the machine itself, that turns out the work.
It is to imply in the case of manual labour, or in those handicrafts
of which manual labour constitutes the chief share, that *nothing
now is virtually done in the tenth hour;* whereas every overlooker or
foreman knows that as a rule only micrometrical measurement
could distinguish between the quantity turned out in the ninth
hour and in the tenth, or in the first as contrasted with the ninth.
It is to imply that labourers habitually proportion their exertions
to the foreseen length of the day ; and that, knowing they will
end their day at the end of nine hours, they do and can work
more efficiently during every one of those nine hours to the degree
of one-ninth or one-tenth. It is to imply that nine hours' labour
leaves a man in the fullest vigour of his working powers, whereas
ten hours' labour impairs those powers to the amount of one-
tenth. Or it implies that hitherto the workman has only put
forth nine-tenths of his productive energies ; or that, determining to earn 5s. a day and no more, he will earn that and that only,
whatever hours he is kept at work. Reasoners practically unacquainted with the management of labour constantly confound two
things essentially distinct ; and argue that because a well-fed
labourer will get through more in nine hours than an ill-fed one will
in ten, therefore among labourers equal in sustenance and strength,
nine hours can be made as productive as ten. They argue further,
that because a man working *by the piece* (*i.e.,* for himself) will do
as much in nine hours as a man *working by the day* (*i.e.,* for his
master) does in ten, therefore men *working alike by the day* will
produce more proportionately as the day is shortened. If ten
hours are as productive as nine, why not eight as nine ? why not
five as six ? why not three as four, and so on ? "

or workmen who consciously do not or are not allowed
to put forth their full energy with others who are
fettered by no such restrictions. Mr Brassey's
chapter on this subject in his "Work and Wages"
does not, I confess, at all shake my conclusion; and
he is so fair a reasoner, and so open to fresh knowledge, that many of the representations in his first
book are largely modified by the far more valuable
address on "Wages in 1873," delivered before the
Social Science Association in that year; while many
passages might be quoted showing his strong sense of
the degree in which our manufacturing position is
menaced by the effect of shorter hours in enhancing
the cost of production of articles in which foreign
competition is imminent.

My next proposition—too certain to be disputed, and
too plain to need any elucidation—is *that diminished
productiveness of labour implies of necessity enhanced
cost of the article produced*, by a double operation;
the machinery of the capitalist as well as the hands
of the labourer being reduced to idleness for a given
length of time; yielding interest only for eight hours
instead of ten. If a given sum in wages, and a given
sum in *plant*, and a further given sum in steam-
power and other contingent expenses (very nearly the
same for eight hours as for ten), have to be spread
over 8000 pieces of calico, or 8000 tons of iron,
instead of 10,000, it is obvious that each piece of
calico and each ton of iron will cost proportionally
more. One only way exists of reducing the quantity

produced without thus enhancing the cost of production. It has been thus succinctly stated :—

"It may be asked, Is it not possible to reduce the hours of labour without thereby thus mischievously enhancing the cost of production, and the price of the article produced ? Unquestionably in many cases it is; but by means which the working man does not contemplate, and at a sacrifice he is little prepared to meet. The aim might be attained, nearly but not quite, if the workmen would be content to receive only *eight hours' wages for eight hours' work*—that is, to be paid at the same rate as now for the amount produced. We say 'nearly, but not quite;'—and the reason of the guarded phrase will be clear from a few moments' consideration. The cost of production of any article consists of two elements—the wages of labour, and what are technically called 'contingent expenses'—*i.e.*, the interest of the capital invested, both fixed and floating, the wear and tear or depreciation of the 'plant' or machinery and buildings, and the outlay on sundry articles used in the processes, such as coal, oil, leather, &c., whose consumption does not bear a strict proportion to the hours of work. Now, these 'contingent expenses' — this second main element in the cost of production—are the same, or nearly the same, whatever be the hours of work ; they are almost as great for eight hours as for twelve, and must be reckoned rather by the year than by the day. The proportion which these bear to mere wages in the calculation of the cost of · the articles produced, varies of course enormously according to the nature of the trade; but probably it is a fair average to reckon that labour constitutes *two-thirds*, and 'contingencies' (interest, &c.), *one-third* of the total. Now, the shorter the hours worked, and consequently the smaller the quantity of goods produced, the heavier will these fixed expenses—this unvarying and inescapable one-third—weigh upon each pound, or yard, or hundredweight of those goods. It is obvious, therefore, that the workman, who determines to work only eight hours, and so limits himself to only eight hours' production, must, in order to prevent the total cost of production being enhanced thereby, content himself, not with eight hours' wages in lieu of ten or twelve, *but with something like seven hours' wages.* This is the condition on which alone he can solve the problem of limiting the hours of labour without mischievously and onerously, and perhaps ruinously, enhancing prices, restricting sales, and sapping the prosperity of the particular industry by which he lives. On no easier terms can he obtain his cherished object; for the laws of economic science, being neither more nor less than the laws of Nature, are stern and unrelenting, and no theorizing or enthusiasm can shake off their grasp."— (*Quarterly Review,* " The Proletariat on a False Scent.")

We desire to express no opinion as to the desirableness of shorter hours of labour generally. They might be a great blessing to the artizans, as to all classes, if they are prepared to pay the needful price for them (which as yet they are not), and if they are qualified and likely to employ the accruing leisure profitably and rationally (of which at present they have shown no signs). We proceed, therefore, to the next step in our reasoning—and maintain that *an increased cost of production must be dangerous and pernicious, and probably fatal to this country;* and will ensure our ultimate shipwreck on that " Rock ahead" which Cassandra already sees looming in the distance.

But before dealing with this argument we must allude to the mischievous operation of some of the more unenlightened proceedings of trades unions in still further increasing the cost of production in this country. These are several — none perhaps very serious taken singly, but in their aggregate effect by no means contemptible. First come various absurd regulations to hinder workmen from putting forth their full strength and skill, lest they should raise the standard of average requirement as against their less qualified fellows (of which the law prevalent among bricklayers of forbidding unionists fully to use both hands in their task may be taken as an extreme sample).*—Next may be specified the analogous and widely-extended discouragement of piece-work, and the systematic endeavour to enforce a uniform rate of wages without reference to the varying capacities of different men and of the quality of their labour—a practice which arose, no doubt, out of some confused notion of fair play or kindness to the weaker brethren, but which a few moments' reflection will show to be cruelly unjust to the more energetic, competent, ambitious, or heavily burdened workman, as well as singularly noxious in diminishing the efficiency of labour, and thereby enhancing the cost of the article to which that labour is applied. The rules, very general at

---

* A pretty full account of these artificial fetters will be found in Mr Thornton's book on "Labour," p. 323, *et seq.* See also Professor Cairnes' " Leading Principles of Political Economy," pp. 307-312. (See Appendix B.)

one time, and still extensively in operation, for limiting the number of apprentices whom each skilled workman was allowed to instruct in his own trade, and the prohibition of any one not regularly apprenticed from practising that trade, operate sensibly in the same direction, and were introduced avowedly for preventing anything like free competition and the effect it was feared it must produce in reducing wages.—All these restrictions—the number and vexatious character of which only those who have studied the subject somewhat in detail can fully estimate— being fetters upon the master's freedom as to the most profitable mode of carrying on his business, add to the necessary cost of manufacture involved, discourage the capitalist, and place him at a disadvantage in the struggle with less hampered rivals. But, worst of all, are the Strikes arising perhaps nearly as often out of these vexatious rules as out of the question of mere wages—strikes which we maintain do eventuate, in nearly every case, on a balance of calculations, in a positive loss to the artizan, but which, whether successful or unsuccessful in their immediate aim, must, it is obvious, equally and necessarily add to the cost of producing the commodity with which they are concerned, whether it be the raising of coal, the weaving of cotton or woollen cloth, the building of houses, or the construction and working of railways.* In all

---

* While these pages are passing through the press, an instructive illustration has been afforded. The strike among the Durham colliers raised the price of coal in London in a single day by 6s. a

strikes, the two great elements of productive industry —the labour of the men and the capital of the master—alike lie idle; for a longer or short time they are as it were annihilated or stricken with paralysis; for weeks or months the industrial capacity of England, *pro tanto* ceases to yield fruit; the articles it is usually occupied in creating for consumption or exchange are therefore reduced in amount by a tenth or a twelfth or a twentieth, and, if they are to continue as remunerative as usual, must be sold at a higher price. Now a higher price, we all know, as a rule means a limited consumption and a curtailed demand. Every strike thus diminishes the wealth of England, often by astonishing, even incalculable, sums. The strike of the miners in South Wales, two years ago, which lasted many weeks, was estimated to have cost upwards of £800,000 in direct loss—a loss divided in various proportions among the masters, the shopkeepers, the Union funds—*i.e.*, *the workmen's savings* —and charitable neighbours.* In fine, if a strike be unsuccessful, it increases indirectly the price of the

---

ton. Indeed, the year 1874 bids fair to be a year of conflict and of strikes, which will waste vast amounts of capital and of earnings, · will teach us many lessons, and clench many of the arguments of this paper.

* "Wages in 1873," p. 6. In this case only £40,000 was recouped to the men out of Union funds. In a previous strike of smaller extent, in the autumn of 1871, which lasted twelve weeks and involved 10,000 men, their losses in wages reached £120,000, of which the union only recouped them £6383, while their masters lost about £150,000. See a long list of cases nearly as serious, collected in Mr Thornton's book " On Labour," p. 230, 293, 296.

article concerned by the waste of interest on the plant of the capitalist, and by the artificial scarcity caused in the supply of the article. If the strike be successful, and do actually raise the rate of wages, it increases the cost of the article in question, not only in the same way and to the same degree as an unsuccessful one, but by the further addition of this enhanced rate. In either case it injures the consumer by making him pay a higher price ; in either case it is injurious to England by causing her to produce at a relatively dearer cost than her rivals. And if these generally higher prices be procured by the operation of strikes in all or in the majority of trades, then the workmen in no trade are benefited by the rise of wages, because all are consumers, and all have to pay more for the commodities they consume.

We beg attention to the following succinct argument, which though published some years since, has never, we believe, been seriously impugned :—

"Though Trades Unions may, and perhaps sometimes do, raise *the rate of wages*, it is by no means clear that they raise the aggregate *earnings* of the workmen, and it is absolutely certain that these earnings are subject, for the maintenance of Trade Unions, to deductions whose total amount would astonish and appal the payers were they to be added up. The contributions levied by more or less compulsion and 'social pressure'—often, as we now learn, by actual outrage—on the members of the Union, range from 5 to 20 per cent. on their weekly earnings ; and how much of these contributions is expended in 'strikes,' in payments to officers, in the hiring of bravoes, and in the maintenance in idleness—*i.e.*, the buying off—of competing applicants for employment, we shall never know with accuracy. But every now and then a few facts leak out, which give us a glimpse of what the truth may be. We know that unemployed workmen will constantly apply for work, and will accept work in nearly all trades at lower wages than those prevalent, unless frightened away or bought off; and that the means resorted to are usually a mixture of these two systems. We are told that in the case of one of the most notorious Unions at Sheffield, the rate of wages has only been kept up at the cost of maintaining ' on the box,' *one-third* of the whole number of those engaged in the trade— *i.e.*, paying them for being idle. In the case of the colliers, many thousands of unemployed men are often thus supported on the earnings of the employed, in order to prevent them from competing; and I am informed on very high authority—indeed, I believe the fact is quite notorious—that in several cases the contributors to this ' buying off' fund are miners who themselves will only work four days a week, and are habitually drunk the other three. Again, some months ago the *Economist* published some very careful, and apparently moderate, calculations of the cost of ' strikes,' as compared with their achievements even when successful, showing that in nearly every case the loss of earnings to the operatives by the time they were on strike, added to the contributions levied upon them for the purpose of enabling them to strike, came to a sum which it would require many years of the enhanced rate of wages to make good. And this was in the case—comparatively rare—of successful strikes. When they fail, of course the loss is total, uncompensated, and often frightful.

" When, therefore, we sum up the matter, and consider, first, the degree to which the cost of every article, and thereby the cost of living in the aggregate, is increased by the operation of Trade Unions; secondly, the diminished demand for labourers consequent upon the limitation of the consumption of the article they produce, caused by the enhancement of its price; thirdly, the heavy tax levied in the form of contributions ' to the box ' on the earnings of the artizans; and fourthly, the encouragement thus given to foreign competition, whereby the demand for British productions, and for the labour of the British workmen, is reduced and endangered—is it not as certain and as plain as anything can be, that Trade Unions are a miscalculation and a gigantic blunder, looked at even from an artizan point of view; and that, on the whole, a more grievous folly never was maintained at a more deplorable cost, or by means more utterly condemnable—alike in defiance of sound economic principles and of the simplest dictates of morality ?"

. . . " If, as I am nearly certain, the *net* average earnings of the individual workman are not increased, and if, as I feel confident, the *aggregate* earnings of the whole body of artizans of each class are not increased, then the working men are losers and not gainers by the Unions. For, even if the Unions do increase *the rate of wages*, and yet (as I maintain) do not increase the *net earnings* of the workmen, they do them a balance of mischief;—*they succeed in raising the price of the articles they have to buy, and they fail in raising the price of the article they have to sell— namely, their labour.*"—(*Political Problems*, p. 124, *et seq.*)

The only other means we need specify by which Trades Unions seek, often successfully, to increase the cost of production, is too plain, and now too notorious, to require anything beyond a mere reference. The colliers are now, under the direction of their leaders, striving directly and avowedly to keep up the late high price of coal, and thus to paralyze the iron trade and injure many other industries, as well as harass every householder throughout the kingdom (the poor far more than the rich)—by artificially restricting the output. No better illustration of the main argument of this paper could be desired. If the colliers could succeed in their scheme, and succeed throughout the kingdom, and succeed continuously, then it is plain that every manufacture, every article of consumption and of export, must be reduced in amount, enhanced in price, cost proportionally more in carriage to the shipping port and in distribution to the home consumer ; the purchasing power of every man's income would be lessened, the exchangeable produce of England deplorably reduced, and her position in relation to rival producers abroad fatally affected.*

III. The unrivalled amount of capital possessed by

---

* On the other point alluded to in the outset, viz., the diminished conscientiousness of British labour, I do not propose to dwell, partly because it is rather notorious than distinctly demonstrative, and partly because the full illustration of it would demand a multitude of details which would encumber the main argument. But there can be no question, I fear, that British workmanship no longer bears throughout the world the unfailing reputation and confidence it once .commanded, nor that our power of defying foreign competition has been in some departments seriously compromised in consequence. The falling-off is discoverable in various branches of housebuilding, in shipbuilding, in the cotton manufacture, and in cutlery. It must, however, be borne in mind that the blame here must fall, in the majority of cases, not on the workman, but on the employer,—on the speculative builder, the fraudulent contractor, the reckless shipowner, the "shoddy" manufacturer, and so on.—It may be well to call to mind here the analogous circumstance that German rivals are in so many quarters beating us out of the field as merchants, by their more untir

the British manufacturer was one of his special advantages in the industrial rivalry with foreign nations.
His command of capital is greater than ever, but it is
no longer his exclusively. For not only are other countries growing rich almost as rapidly as England; not only
is the wealth of Germany and Italy augmenting fast;
not only is America in ordinary years *making* as much
money as we are, and France *saving* perhaps more;
but British capital is at the command of the American,
the French, the Italian, and the German manufacturer
almost as freely, and more than as profitably, as at that
of the Englishman. In truth, any country that wishes
for capital and can use it well, may have it for the
asking. Here, then, our peculiar advantage is gone,
as in other elements of cheap production we have
shown that it is going.

---

ing patience, industry, enterprise, and thrift. " The papers lately
teemed with letters and articles proving and accounting for the
facts, that our merchant princes had discovered competitors in all
their branches of commerce, who could afford to undersell them in
their own trade, and in their own markets; and that foreigners,
not content with rivalling our great houses in our colonies and
possessions abroad, were settling in our very midst, and securing
to themselves the cream of our own business in England. The
fact was brought home to us that many a lucrative field of commercial enterprise was being taken from us by the personal thrift
and frugality, by the dogged perseverance, and even by the dash-
ing speculation of foreigners. Our Germanic neighbours have
been accused of supplanting us in Asia and South America; the
Greeks of monopolising the corn trade of the Black Sea; the
French of ousting us from the Levant and Mediterranean, leaving
us the doubtful glory of inventing means by which our export
goods are more cheaply produced, but which have not redounded
to our commercial honour or credit."—*Capital and Labour.*

We have now reached that stage in our argument when we may fitly cast a glance round and point to a few indications that the successful foreign competition —which we have announced as menacing our industry in the future, in consequence of the increasing cost of production in this country,—is no mere dream, or even logical inference, or distant and problematic contingency, but an actual fact, visible and approaching, and not very far off. Here, as hitherto, I shall merely *refer* to proofs and details—not transfer them to these pages. They are not very many; they are not perhaps very strong or startling; but they are indisputable, and they are significant.

1. The high price of coal, coupled with Union action to keep up the inflated wages of last year, have already caused the " blowing out " or "damping down" of a vast number of iron furnaces and rolling mills, and enabled Belgian iron-masters to secure large spring orders for rails, &c., which were offered to English makers in the first instance. Every week's newspapers in March and April contained announcements of this nature. Here, then, is an instance in which the foreseen mischief has been already realised. Nor is Belgium our only rival. Prussia and America* are

---

* The gigantic works of Messrs Krupp, at Essen, are now to be enlarged by the expenditure of a million of money in new *plant,*— and this at a time when our iron industry is under a cloud. Very recently a Small Arms Company in the United States carried off an order for a million sterling in the face of both British and Belgian competition.—It is well known, too, that our chief machine-makers are principally engaged upon Continental and

extensively both iron-producing and iron-working countries, and supply themselves with articles which formerly they procured from England.

2. Mr Lowthian Bell in his Presidential Address to
the Iron · and Steel Institute (Journal, Vol. I., 1873,
p. 32), says :—

"During a journey, undertaken about five years ago,
with Mr John Lancaster, through a great number of mines
and ironworks in France, Belgium, and Prussia, we came
to the following conclusion :—In many instances, the iron-
masters on this side of the water were paying at that time
nearly double the wages given abroad for similar work.
Notwithstanding this—owing to the magnitude of our ironworks, to the superiority of our arrangements for economising labour, and to the greater amount of work done by
individuals—the nett disadvantage was reduced to a
difference in favour of the foreign makers of about 25 per
cent. The extent of this drawback, however, has been
greatly magnified by the recent alterations in the scale of
wages paid in this kingdom ; for while ours will probably
average 50 per cent. on the old rates, theirs do not exceed
10 to 20 per cent., so that in point of relative position,
labour costing on the Continent 20s. will here amount to
30s. or 35s."*

3. A great amount of valuable information as to
our competitors in various textile fabrics may be found

American orders for machinery, all of which will be worked by
our competitors for longer hours than those to which we are even
now restricted.

* "Wages in 1873," p. 26.   " Of late " (says Mr Brassey, p.
30) " the cost of building first-class steamers and marine engines
has risen in England from 30 to 40 per cent."

in the two volumes of Reports from our Secretaries of
Legation in Belgium, Switzerland, Germany, and the
United States, which were presented to Parliament in
1873.* From these it appears that in cotton at least,
if not in woollens, the United States expect ere long
to surpass us, though prevented by heavy taxation and
high-priced labour from doing so at present. In some
heavy goods we know that years ago, before the war,
they exported largely and successfully to foreign
markets (occasionally beating us in "drills" and
" domestics ")—and doubtless will do so again.
German hosiery undersells English in America, and
is we believe sometimes sent to England. Belgium
has increased her exports of woollen yarns *sixfold* in
the last ten years, and of these exports *more than half
come to this country*; as does also about one-quarter
of her woollen cloths. She sends flax yarn also to
Ireland. One cotton mill at Ghent is entirely
engaged in producing for the English market. But
perhaps Switzerland is our most formidable rival in
continental countries. She is increasing her factories
at a rapid pace, and already exports largely both to
Italy and Germany.†

---

* Thirty years ago we had 850,000 flax spindles, and the Continent not 200,000. Now we have 1,503,000, and the Continent
1,722,000. In the Cotton trade our spindles now are reckoned at
36,000,000, those of Europe and the United States together about
28,000,000.

† Mr Brassey says, " Wages in 1873," p. 50 : " It has been
already pointed out that in England we have to contend against
competition of two kinds—against the cheaper labour of the Continent on the one side, and against the superior natural resources

4. It is notorious that in nearly every branch of manufacture and machine-making, the most successful and serviceable inventions have for many years been of American origin.*

5. But the great salient facts bearing on the subject are these :—Other countries, already rival producers and manufacturers, *can raise coal as cheap as ours, and contain incomparably richer deposits.*†

of America on the other. While we occupy at the present time a highly favoured position, which has been attained not merely by the skill of our workmen, but by the administrative skill of their employers, and the gradual accumulation of an ample capital in their hands, the race with other great manufacturing countries is very close. The Swiss have entered into competition with our own manufacturers, both in the home and foreign trades. The exports of textile fabrics from Switzerland, as we learn from Mr Gould's report, have risen from £12,485,000 in 1860, to £26,464,000 in 1871, an advance of 112½ per cent. In this total the exports to the United States have risen from £509,000 in 1862, to £2,159,000 in 1872, in other words, over 324 per cent. In cheap silks and ribbons the Swiss are able to compete with the British producer in the English market ; and, to sum up the case in the words of Mr Gould, 'The advantages of Switzerland in competition with Great Britain are the use of water power as a substitute for steam power to the extent of upwards of 80 per cent., low wages, long hours of labour, and a minimum expenditure for management.' On the other hand, as an inland country, Switzerland has to pay heavy freights, the workmen are inferior in activity to our own, buildings for machinery are more costly, and from want of capital, production is on a smaller scale than here. The balance, however, seems to be greatly in favour of Switzerland, and cannot fail to become greater from day to day."

* "Wages in 1873," p. 26.

† "So far as the actual cost of extraction is concerned, I make no doubt that at the present day in France, Prussia, and Belgium, coal on an average can be as cheaply delivered at the pit's mouth as it is in this country."—*President's Address, Journal of Iron and Steel Institute,* vol. i., 1873, p. 32.

The area of the American coal-fields exceeds that of
British coal-fields in the ratio of 37 to 1, and the
following are the comparative prices of coal at the
pit's mouth in the various countries :—*

France	.	.	.	6s. to 14s.
Germany	.	.	.	7 10
England	.	.	.	6 10
Pensylvania	.	.	8 9
Pittsburg	.	.	.	2 4

The following account by Sir C. Lyell † completes
the picture of the advantages of our most formidable
rival :—

" On the west of the Alleghany Mountains, the coal
measures are intersected by three great navigable rivers,
*and are capable of supplying for ages, to the inhabitants of a
densely peopled region, an inexhaustible supply of fuel.* All
these rivers *lay open on their banks the level seams of coal·*
Looking down the first of these at Brownsville, we have a
fine view of the main seam of bituminous coal, ten feet
thick, commonly called the Pittsburg seam, breaking out in
the steep cliff at the water's edge. Horizontal galleries
may be driven everywhere at very slight expense, and so
worked as to drain themselves ; while the cars, laden with
coal and attached to each other, glide down on a railway,
so as to deliver their burdens into barges moored to the
river's bank. The same seam is seen at a distance on the right
bank, and may be followed the whole way to Pittsburg, fifty
miles off. As it is nearly horizontal, while the river descends,
it crosses out at a continually increasing, but never incon-
venient height above the Monongahela. Below the great bed

---

* " The Coal Question," by W. S. Jevons, pp. 266-270.
" Manual of Elementary Geology," p. 331.

coal at Brownsville is a fire-clay, 18 inches thick, and below this several ı beds · of limestone, below which, again, are other coal seams. . . . Here almost every proprietor can open a coal-pit on his own land, and the stratification being very regular, he may calculate with precision the depth at which coal will be won."*

The various facts and considerations marshalled above seem to me conclusive. Do not let us be · deluded into deceptive security by being told that our manufactures are increasingly swelling in extent, and that our exports continue even to countries which we are told are, or soon will be, successful rivals. The

---

* " If then," says the President of the Iron and Steel Institute, than whom no higher authority can be cited (Journal," vol. i., 1873, p. 33 ; see also p. 229), " we have to apprehend the advent of a powerful rival in the iron trade, it is not, unless new coal discoveries are made, the old world of Europe we have to fear, but the immense and undoubted powers possessed by the western hemisphere. In ores of the finest descriptions, the resources of the United States are unlimited, while in coal our own wealth is, in comparison, but poverty. In many cases, the relative geographical situation of these minerals is not unfavourable ; in short, there is apparently but one bar to a boundless production of iron in the New World—that of human hands to manufacture it. The stream of emigrants, however, constantly flowing from this side of the Atlantic, would seem to enable our friends on the other to advance at a rate unknown even in this country ; for according to the 'Statistical Report of the National Association of Iron Manufactures,' of the United States, no less than 107 furnaces were erected there in 1872, which is equal to an increase of 18 per cent. of those in blast in 1870. In the matter of skill, everyone who has had the opportunity of inspecting the American ironworks concurs in reporting that their development is quite in keeping with the advantages Nature has conferred upon that highly-favoured country."

facts are so; but properly considered they in no way militate against my conclusions. I speak of causes in operation, not of effects completed or as yet largely visible—of results that must come and are slowly coming, not of *faits accomplis.* Our exports, continue to increase, because the demands of the world are increasing; because even the countries which can produce more cheaply than we do can as yet not quite meet even their own home requirements; because, as in the United States, a fallacious commercial policy is fettering their hands; because labour is as yet scarce; because in many quarters the application of capital to the development of native resources is in its infancy or its struggling youth. But if my premises are sound and uncontrovertible, these exports must in time, *first,* cease to augment at the same rapid ratio as heretofore, then cease to augment at all, then gradually, and perhaps speedily fall off.

Since this argument was first published, several critics have eagerly protested against my conclusions, not, however, as logically unwarranted by my premises, but as too gloomy for the mind to be able to admit in the glare of sunshine now around us. Two of these protests I must notice before I proceed. It is urged, " that England's *relative* manufacturing decline need involve nothing positive in its nature, but may even be compatible with a large and continuous increase in her aggregate production; that the demand of the whole globe may, and probably will, advance more rapidly than it can be supplied by

the united industries of our cheaper rivals ; that we
therefore shall be still called upon to meet the deficiency ;—and that thus our total exports may go on
and even swell, long after our manufacturing 'supremacy' (*i.e.*, productive advantages and superiority)
shall have been lost." Granted ;—but in this case
England, in place of manufacturing for nearly the
whole world, will manufacture only for a portion of it ;
she will have only her share, instead of twenty times
more than her share as hitherto ; instead of having
the pick of the orders of the globe, she will have to be
content with the *refuse;*—other nations, producing
more cheaply than she can, will have the preference
in the market, and will reap larger profits, which
larger profits again will so stimulate their productiveness, as infallibly ere long to edge her out altogether.
In fact, orders will go to the country that can execute
them most cheaply, which country must end. as soon
as her development is advanced enough, in executing
them all; and that country, *ceteris paribus*, will
be the one which has the cheapest iron and the
cheapest coal. All, therefore, that the most rapid
progress in the needs and consumption of the globe
can do, is not to negative or frustrate my prophecy,
but to postpone the date of its realisation. Cottons,
woollens, rails, machinery, will be produced as heretofore, and in overflowing measure ; they may be even
produced by Englishmen, or by men of English race,
as now,—but they will be produced by them, not in
Lancashire, Staffordshire, Lanarkshire, or Yorkshire,

but on the banks of the Ohio, at the foot of the Alleghany, or it may be even in more distant quarters still.
Further, it is argued that I have formed a very
inadequate conception of the coming expansion of the
commerce of the world, of the opening of entirely
new markets, and the removal of fetters which restrict
our exports to the old ones. "Conceive," it is said, "the
vast demand which would at once spring up for our iron,
cottons, woollens, machinery, &c., were the United States
at once and for good to reverse their suicidal prohibitive
fiscal system, and the further orders which will pour
into our markets as soon as the new spirit of the
Japanese shall have definitively assumed the upper
hand. We may then look for a sudden prosperity
(even to the extent of inflation) which will be almost
demoralising, and which will banish all your dark
forebodings to the winds." I reply that such a sudden
and genuine, and to a certain extent durable burst of .
prosperity is very possible, to say no more; and that
it may drown the sound of my forebodings is likely
enough, but it will confirm rather than disperse them,
and will hasten and ensure their realisation. For the
operations of such a burst most confidently to be
counted upon, would be, *first*, a far more reckless
consumption and more rapid exhaustion of our coal;
secondly, a further enhancement of the wages of our
artisans, and a shortening of their hours of labour,
both combined raising the cost of production of all
articles required; and *thirdly*, the discountenancing
of that faint anxiety about the future which is just

dawning, and which a period of adversity might possibly consolidate and fix; and a renewed course of
blind self-indulgence more careless even, and more
noxious, than before.

Our conclusion, then, we maintain to have been
logically established by irrefragable data, and the summary of those data is as follows :—

The basis of our industrial supremacy—the one
special advantage which has made our country the
workshop of the world—is beyond question *cheap*
coal; and coal is ceasing to be cheap—*must* cease to
be cheap, relatively and positively—must become
dearer and dearer year by year, long before the stage
of actual exhaustion is even approached—nay, did last
year, as by way of warning of what may be, reach a
point of dearness at which the great industries of
England were menaced with paralysis.   The day
when the advantage of cheap coal shall be lost to us
for ever must therefore arrive;—economy may retard, but cannot hinder its arrival;—if we begin
and continue to reduce consumption steadily and at
once, it will come late—if we do not, it will come
soon;—and we shall apparently only be driven to
those economising contrivances and habits which will
keep it cheap by its becoming or remaining dear.
Other countries—notably our most formidable rival,
the United States—have supplies of coal incomparably
larger than our own, and can raise that coal at a
decidedly lower cost;—and coal is at once so indispensable, so primary, and so bulky an article, that it

transfers the industrial sceptre of the world to the land where it is found in the greatest abundance and at the lowest price.

The second great advantage which has hitherto made us the workshop of the world—the efficiency and conscientiousness of our artisans—is becoming distinctly impaired by operations the influence of which is notorious, and the cure or counteraction of which is not yet visible. The power and the organization of our working classes are growing year by year, and that power and organization are being persistently applied to obtain higher rates of wages, and to enforce shorter hours of labour, while that labour is from the same causes becoming less conscientious and less disciplined. The inevitable result of these combined agencies is that the cost of production of the commodities for which Great Britain has always been most famous, is greatly enhanced both positively and relatively; while the boundless concentration and command of capital, which hitherto have so enormously reduced that relative cost are no longer exclusively her own.

Stated thus cautiously and moderately, our data cannot be gainsaid; nor can the inference we deduce from them, it would appear, be controverted or invalidated by the hardiest disputant. That inference is briefly this :—that gradually, inevitably, ere long (I abstain resolutely from suggesting any date), as the productions of our industry grow positively more costly, the demand for them will be proportionally curtailed ;—that as they grow more costly here rela-

G

tively to the expense of producing them in other countries, those countries will supply themselves and their neighbours instead of purchasing them from us; —that our manufacturing exports will receive a check, will dwindle, eventually, perhaps may -even cease;—in fact (to state it broadly), that in place of manufacturing for all the world, we may come to manufacture only for ourselves.*

Of course, as soon as this tendency becomes so perceptible as to be undeniable we shall take alarm; antagonistic agencies will come into play, and antagonistic efforts will be made. Coal, ceasing to be in such demand, will fall in price; the lower price will stimulate coalowners to inventions directed to economise the cost of raising it; colliers, being less sought after, will become redundant, and will ultimately (after fierce recalcitration and many wasteful strikes) accept lower wages;—artizans in the iron trade, the cotton trade, and the rest, finding that far fewer of them are needed, will perforce be content with scantier earnings, and will be anxious to work longer hours. *But all these consequences will flow only from the pressure of that adversity which I am predicting;*—will not be submitted to till that

---

* Of course it is possible that competing nations may be as foolish as ourselves, following our suicidal footsteps in the shape of strikes, inflated wages, shorter hours, and exhausting conflicts between the two great productive powers, Capital and Labour; and may thus retard our comparative decline. But if their artizans are no wiser than ours, their governments, so far, at least, are stronger.

pressure is painfully felt;—*may* not be submitted to till the mischief is done, possibly not till it is past repair. By the time the danger is undeniable it will have grown irremediable.

This last sentence comprises the critical question for England's future. I do not feel that we can venture on any prophecy regarding it—scarcely perhaps upon any confident conjecture. Much— nearly everything, it may be—depends upon whether the people of England can be persuaded that the above gloomy prognostics are correct, and whether, when so persuaded, they will have sagacity, resolution, and self-denial to take the necessary steps to avert the peril, to take those steps in time, and to persevere in them with steady sternness. I see no reason to believe that they can be so persuaded, or that they will so act. Of course, on the one hand, *if* they were at once to introduce all available economies in the use of coal, all new contrivances for its less costly raising, and all needed reductions of wages, coal would soon so fall in price and would remain so low, as to restore to us for a period, possibly for a long period, our pristine advantage. *If*, again, artizans of all classes, awakening to their danger, were at once to abandon those practices and follies which have brought danger upon them, to eschew all strikes, to abandon all artificial fetters upon industry, to become once more subordinate and conscientious, to work for whatever hours and to be content with whatever rate of wages might prove indispensable to keep the cost of pro-

duction in our staple industries as low as heretofore;
—then, no doubt, our menaced manufacturing
supremacy might be preserved indefinitely, though
not perpetually. But, on the other hand, coal must
never—can never—fall so low as to leave no adequate profit on the working of our mines, or coal
will cease to be raised;—and, as we have seen, there
is good ground for concluding that the prices which
prevailed for some years previous to 1873 were
scarcely remunerative, and cannot therefore be expected to recur for a continuance. It is certain, too,
that America has stores of fuel more accessible and
inexhaustible by far than ours, and which need only a
sufficient supply of labour (which is yearly increasing
already) to be permanently and materially cheaper
than with us. It is certain, moreover, that our
operatives and artizans will not be driven to be more
disciplined and amenable, to work longer hours, and
to be content with lower wages, *except under the
unmistakable pressure of adversity:* and "adversity"
here means that the tide has already turned, that our industrial supremacy is passing from us, that the demand
for the labour of our artizans is diminishing, that their
numbers are redundant—in fact, that their hour has
struck. Commercial affairs flow for long in old
channels, run long in old ruts; but when once they
begin to leave the old ways, the new current they
have chosen is not easily arrested or turned back. I
fear, therefore, that the ultimate industrial decline
of Great Britain is inevitable, and that its approach

will not be made as tardy, or its progress as slow as it might be, were it foreseen as clearly, believed in as fully, and fought against as energetically and sagaciously as I have in these pages striven to bring about.

Now, let us face boldly and state in the plainest language what the industrial decadence of our country, whether it comes sooner or later, will mean when it arrives—will in a great measure mean when it begins. (Statistics are unnecessary here : they cannot be precise, and might give rise to useless controversy on details). It means that we shall lose one foreign market after ·another ; that we shall gradually cease to manufacture for other manufacturing countries ; then that those countries, after supplying themselves, will meet us and beat us in neutral markets ; finally that we shall be reduced to the supply of our home demand—possibly to secure even that market by recurrence to a Protectionist Policy. This will be a terrible reverse—a momentous, and it may be a miserable, change. It *must* involve a vast and grave metamorphosis ; it *may*, but it *need not* involve ruin. The extent and depth of suffering we shall have to undergo during the sad progress and the weary struggle will depend upon how soon and how distinctly we recognise the coming revolution, and how wisely and courageously we meet it.

The great, ultimate, naked fact we have to look at is this :—The home demand for our iron, cotton, woollen goods, &c., may be about one-third of the whole; we manufacture mainly for foreign consumption. About one-third of all our productive industry is therefore all that we can hope ultimately to keep going Two-thirds of our artizan population, therefore, must cease to be—or to remain. That vast proportion of our imports, which is now paid for by our millions of exports, will have to be foregone, or to be purchased by other funds. To speak broadly, the population of these islands which is now maintained by agriculture, commerce, and manufactures, will have to be maintained by agriculture and commerce almost alone.* We shall, therefore, only be able to support 20,000,000 people instead of 30,000,000, as at present. England will become a second Holland, greater, richer, more powerful than the first. But she may be a prosperous and happy Holland still, if only she sees her destiny in time, and girds up her loins to meet it as a great nation should.

---

* Some sanguine controversialists, delirious with past profits and dreaming confidently of their permanence, reply, " Never mind ! Commerce alone will suffice ; we shall always be the favoured and unapproachable carriers for the entire globe, as well as the emporium of its products." This blind trust in our ships and sailors, and merchants, is somewhat wild, but it might pass were the carrying trade of the world now conducted by wooden sailing vessels, and not by iron steamers. But it will seem curiously misplaced when we reflect that cheap iron and cheap coal are precisely the two critical pre-requisites of cheap ships, low freights, and rapid passages ; and that the very foundation of my argument is the on-coming loss by Great Britain of these two possessions.

To secure this sort of national euthanasia—or, to speak more soberly, to smooth the difficulties, avert the perils, and minimize the distress consequent on the vast change from a condition of rapid and exulting progress to that "stationary state" which Mr Mill eulogises in one of the most original chapters he ever wrote—is, it seems to me, by no means impossible if only all classes employ the accorded interval in preparing for the change in a becoming spirit, and begin that preparation in time. The change may perhaps be distant yet; it may be gradual even when it comes. But, however gradual, if not foreseen, and (in plan at least) provided for, suffering must begin as soon as the turn of the tide begins, and may even be the greater and the more prolonged for the very slowness of the ebbing tide; for the ebb, if gentle, will scarcely be at first believed in. But as soon as our production surpasses the demand for our manufactured goods, there must, it would seem, set in a period of curtailed profits, of positive loss where there had been gain, of falling wages, and of painful, costly, angry struggles to prevent the inevitable fall—a period, in short, of that distress to all parties concerned which we have known occasionally as a temporary evil, but never as a permanent fate.

The means of meeting the issue we foresee, so as to suffer as little as we may, and to be left still as nationally strong and healthy as we can, have, most of them, been already hinted at. In the first place, we may postpone the date at which the tide must

turn—that is, we may prolong the interval of preparation for the evil day—by immediate economy in the
use of fuel and in the cost of getting it; by abandoning all those foolish fetters and fatally disastrous
strifes which so swell the expenses of production ; and
by transforming the present contest for shorter hours
of labour into a generous effort to make the labour of
those hours as efficient and conscientious as we can.
Next, the artizan classes must save the £90,000,000
a-year which, as we showed in Part I., they virtually waste ; and must employ the sum so secured,
—*either* in neutralizing the increased cost of production which otherwise must follow from reduced hours
of work, by voluntarily accepting lower wages,* if they
deem (as they well may) leisure to be worth this
price ;—*or* in becoming capitalists and proprietors, as
they may, so as to be able to dispense with daily
earnings during periods of temporary pressure, and
deliberately to ascertain the best field whither to
transfer their industry and their means, as soon as the
pressure becomes evidently permanent ;—and at the
same time must so mend their habits and cultivate
their intelligence that when the trial we foresee shall
overtake them, they may know what they ought to
do, and be in a position to be able to do what they
ought. The exhaustion of our industrial advantages
and the consequent loss of our industrial supremacy,
if it meets a *prepared* manufacturing class—that is, a

---

* See supra, p. 49.

body of operatives and artizans qualified by intellectual training to comprehend the real state of affairs and prospects, and able (by virtue of habits of sobriety and money in the bank) to act in such sagacious manner as that state of affairs distinctly points out to them— may be nothing more than a crisis calling for especial energy and fortitude. ' The same industrial exhaustion and decline, meeting a class of mere proletariat artizans, given to drink, with no property and no savings, untrained to self-denial, and with little in- struction meriting the name,—will be a *catastrophe*, not a *crisis;* will be, must be, simply ruin, alike to themselves and to the nation that has neglected them, ignored them, endured them, pampered them. The day must come : everything depends upon the state in which it finds us when it comes. It lies with us to decide that state still;—a little more sleep, and a little more slumber, and a little more folding of the hands to rest,—a little more pausing in apathy or wrangling in factious strife, as we have been doing Session after Session and Parliament after Parliament, —a little more wasting, in the divisions of intestine parties, the precious moments which should be given to united action,—and the decision will be given over to other hands. Consequences follow causes with inexorable logic. God gives us warnings—visible, audible, timely, and for the most part startling and unmistakable enough ; but He never stays his steps to look whether we have taken them.

The case is very clear, and may be stated very

briefly. England, Europe even, is not the world. The manufacturing industry of the world will not slacken, nor the demand for the products of that industry. On the contrary, we may count upon its continuous and rapid development. As one field of employment closes or is exhausted, others open in profusion in other lands, and labour must leave the failing ones to seek the richer ones opening elsewhere. All that is essential is that the transfer from the old scenes to the new should be easy, and should be timely. Labourers and artizans will grow redundant here, but America, Australia, and New Zealand are clamouring and starving for them. Those countries have vast resources to be called forth : we have the industrious hands, soon no longer to be wanted or provided for here, which can call them forth. Ireland may here be left out of calculation ; partly because a continuous stream of emigration has long since been organized from that island, which is reducing her annual numbers at probably a rapid rate enough ; partly because she is not largely manufacturing, and therefore will be comparatively little affected by the future influences we are considering. But England and Scotland have now a population of 26 millions, and, when the operation which Cassandra anticipates shall be complete, will not be able to support in comfort more than (say) 19 millions. Moreover the natural increase of the population (the surplus of births over deaths) is 300,000 a-year, and will be more ; for neither marriage nor multiplication is likely to be checked, while the average length of life is in regular process of advance, and will still further advance as sanitary improvements prevail. We have, therefore, within a certain number of years or generations—that is, between 1874 and that uncertain period when Great Britain shall have lost her manufacturing supremacy—to export not only our annual increase of about 350,000 souls, but by degrees a further number of about 7,000,000. No doubt this may be done. No doubt it must be done, if the contemplated metamorphosis—from a mainly manufacturing country to a commercial and agricultural one—is to pass over us without grievous suffering. If our people will emigrate as. fast as they become redundant, the grinding wretchedness of gathering redundancy may be avoided. Thus we may escape the worst perils of the coming change. One evil remains, the way of escape from which I confess I do not see ; *—in all emigration that is not official and either assisted or forced, it is the energetic and capable who go, and the lazy and inefficient who remain behind. During the long weary process, therefore, we shall be losing the best of our artizan and agricultural population, and keeping the worst.

---

* Possibly, some mitigation to this mischief may be found by a bargain with the colonies to accept those able-bodied paupers whom we undertake to land *gratis* on their shores. And when the pressure comes, we shall probably come to this common-sense conclusion, that if we consent to support able-bodied men at all, we are at least entitled to support them *wherever* and *however* we please.

So far we have spoken only of the artizan and pro-
letaire classes. Let us now devote a few paragraphs
to the operation of the anticipated reverse of Great
Britain's relative position—when it is completed, and
while it is in process—on the men of property. We
need to speak very briefly on this head; for the facts
are obvious as soon as they are pointed out. Of
course thousands will emigrate, and will carry their
capital with them to rising countries and to richer
fields. Of course thousands more will remain, and in
various branches of commerce—many of them as
merchant princes — will continue to enrich their
country and themselves. Thousands more—perhaps
one-third as many as at present—will continue to
supply the home demand for metallic and textile
manufactures, and to make respectable profits by
doing so. Three other things will remain also—and
this is what chiefly concerns our present purpose—the
land, with the landowners; the Poor Rate, and the
paupers; taxation, and the National Debt.

Eight years ago, in his memorable Budget Speech
of May 3, 1866, Mr Gladstone warned the landowners of England of the fate that was probably in
store for them,* and well do I remember watching the

---

* "Suppose, then, that pre-eminence in the cheap production
of coal should be carried from us away across the Atlantic, what
will happen in that event? There will, probably, be a decline of
rents, a decline of profits, a decline of wages. There will be precisely the reverse of that which we have all seen taking place
within our time—an increase of rents, an increase of profits, an
increase of wages. And when rents, profits, and wages decline,

cloud of perplexity and helpless dismay that spread
over their faces as they listened. I will put the
matter into moderate and indisputable figures.
Unless the Debt be vastly diminished while our sunshine of prosperity continues, the revenue we shall
have to raise will probably not be much smaller than
at present — £70,000,000 ; for the army, navy,
judicature, and civil services needed for twenty
millions of people, so far as we can foresee, will be
nearly the same as are required for thirty. But say
that necessity compels us to be content with only
£60,000,000. Those sixty millions will be levied on
a population reduced by one-third—on a Schedule D
diminished by one-half, on railway profits probably
reduced in proportion, on incomes from Consols possibly endangered, on landed incomes curtailed by a
lowering of rents and of saleable value, the extent of
which we have no means of estimating, but which must

---

what will those interested in them do? Those who receive wages,
finding that wages are lower here than across the Atlantic, will do
in a still greater degree what they even now do somewhat extensively under the attraction of increased and more certain gains,—
will emigrate ; and the holders of moveable property, finding that
there is a wider and more profitable field for the employment of
their capital elsewhere, will send their capital abroad. What will
the owners of rents do? It appears pretty plain that they cannot
migrate. Personally they may do so, but that from which they
derive their income cannot migrate : it is rooted in the soil. The
upshot will be that the charge of the National Debt, which is now
borne in full on property, profits, and rents, and in a very liberal
proportion by the two latter, will remain as a permanent
mortgage in its full force, on the lands, houses, and works of the
country."

be serious, considering that ten millions of the existing competitors for land and landed produce will have gone beyond the seas—on an aggregate of property, in short, every item of which will be far smaller than at present. The burden of taxation, instead of being 40s. a head, will be 60s.; and instead of fourteen per cent. on the income, is will be nearer thirty per cent.[*]

But this is not all. The twenty-four millions of working classes are estimated to pay of the general taxation of the country—now that the sugar tax is gone—about £24,000,000. When more than one-third of these have emigrated (as we have shown they must do), the remaining two-thirds, even if they consume as much of dutiable articles as at present, will only pay £16,000,000 :—and as they will probably be poorer, and, it is to be hoped, wiser, soberer, and less reckless (upwards of twenty millions of our revenue being derived from drink), the consumption of exciseable liquors will fall off, and the deficiency to be made up by property will be, not eight millions, but twelve at least.[†]   In fact, the share of the whole sixty millions which will fall on property will probably be five-sixths, while proletairism will get off for one-sixth.   And the aggregate property which will

---

[*] " Political Problems," ch. xii.

[†] It will then be seen whether our recent dealings with indirect taxation have not been wanting in due foresight ; leaving, as they do, nearly twenty-five millions dependent on articles, the consumption of which we are all trying and hoping to reduce, and which must fall off *pari passu* with the mental and moral improvement of the people.

be thus heavily hit, will be far less than it is now. The prospect is not cheering ; exception may be taken to some of the figures ; but we cannot conceive that any discussion which accepts the basis of the argument can materially invalidate the unwelcome conclusion.

Even this, however, does not exhaust all that is gloomy in the picture of our apparent future. Local taxation must also be taken into our account. We see no reason why its amount should diminish, and several reasons why it should increase. Highway rates, police rates, sanitary rates, will remain, while the Poor Rate, it would seem, must inevitably be augmented—if, indeed, more philosophic legislation have not by that time swept it away. We know of no case in which decaying trade and fading manufactures have not brought about swelling pauperism. The redundant population will have to remove to other lands ; but it will not remove as fast as it becomes redundant, and the process of removal will be costly, as well as tedious and tardy ; while the poor whom it leaves will in all likelihood be more helpless as well as more numerous than now. The ten millions which we may under severe pressure economise from our general revenue, it is more than likely we may have to add to our local burdens. And all these things, be it remembered, are not conjectural merely, but certain, *if* cheap fuel does lie at the basis of our industrial supremacy, and *if* fuel must cease, and is ceasing, to be cheap.

It would be too painful to end the chapter with a scroll so written all over with lamentation and woe.

Let us try to gather a farewell gleam of comfort by a glance at that "Stationary State" to which it would appear we must come in time, and which, though reached probably through much tribulation, may be the reverse of disastrous when attained. This glance will be best given in the words of a great man recently departed from among us,*—premising only that the result which he looked for to systematic restraint upon the increasing numbers of the population, I look for to the systematic and timely removal of those increasing numbers to more productive and less crowded fields:—

"I cannot regard the stationary state of capital and wealth with the unaffected aversion so generally manifested towards it by political economists of the old school. I am inclined to believe that it would be, on the whole, a very considerable improvement on our present condition. I confess I am not charmed with the ideal of life held out by those who think that the normal state of human beings is that of struggling to get on; that the trampling, crushing, elbowing, and treading on each other's heels, which form the existing type of social life, are the most desirable lot of human kind, or anything but the disagreeable symptoms of one of the phases of industrial progress. The Northern and Middle States of America are a specimen of this stage of civilization in very favourable circumstances; having, apparently, got rid of all social injustices and inequalities that affect persons of Caucasian race and of the male sex; while the proportion of population to capital and land is such as to ensure abundance to every able-bodied member of the community who does not forfeit it by misconduct. They have the six points of Chartism, and they have no poverty;

* "Principles of Political Economy," by J. S. Mill, book iv., ch. vi.

and all that these advantages do for them is that the life of
the whole of one sex is devoted to dollar-hunting, and of
the other to breeding dollar-hunters. This is not a kind of
social perfection which philanthropists to come will feel any
very eager desire to assist in realising. . . .

" It is only in the backward countries of the world that
increased production is still an important object: in those
most advanced, what is economically needed is a better distribution, of which an indispensable means is a stricter
restraint on population. Levelling institutions, either of a
just or of an unjust kind, cannot alone accomplish it ; they
may lower the heights of society, but they cannot raise the
depths.

" There is room in the world, no doubt, and even in old
countries, for an immense increase of population, supposing
the arts of life to go on improving, and capital to increase.
But, although it may be innocuous, I confess I see very
little reason for desiring it. The density of population
necessary to enable mankind to obtain, in the greatest degree, all the advantages both of co-operation and of social
intercourse, has, in all the more populous countries, been
attained. A population may be too crowded, though all
be amply supplied with food and raiment. It is not good
for man to be kept perforce at all times in the presence of
his species. A world from which solitude is extirpated is a
very poor ideal. Solitude, in the sense of being often alone,
is essential to any depth of meditation or of character ; and
solitude, in the presence of natural beauty and grandeur, is
the cradle of thoughts and aspirations which are not only
good for the individual, but which society could ill do without. Nor is there much satisfaction in contemplating the
world with nothing left to the spontaneous activity of
nature ; with every rood of land brought into cultivation
which is capable of growing food for human beings ; every

H

flowery waste or natural pasture ploughed up ; all quadru-
peds or birds which are not domesticated for man's use
exterminated as his rivals for food ; every hedgerow or
superfluous tree rooted out, and scarcely a place left where
a wild shrub or flower could grow without being eradicated
as a weed in the name of improved agriculture. If the
earth must lose that great portion of its pleasantness which
it owes to things that the unlimited increase of wealth and
population would extirpate from it, for the mere purpose of
enabling it to support a larger, but not a better or a happier
population, I sincerely hope, for the sake of posterity, that
they will be content to be stationary, long before necessity
compels them to it."

III.

RELIGIOUS ROCK.

III.

THE religion of a nation ought to be the embodiment of its highest Intelligence in the most solemn moments of that Intelligence. It should be—if not the outcome, at least in harmony with the outcome—of the deepest thoughts, the richest experience, the widest culture, the finest intuitions of the best and wisest minds that nation counts among its children. This is not to say that it need be the *discovery* or the elaborated produce of the nation's intellect working by itself without guidance or without illumination; for most among us hold religion to be an external gift, a matter of authoritative communication from on high—a revelation, in short, dealing with topics which transcend man's natural capacities; and many who do not accept this, the ordinary view, still admit it to be more or less the issue of those gifted moments of gifted men whose untraced suggestions, intuitions, spontaneous conceptions of the inner spirit, reach very near to something which may be vaguely spoken of as Inspiration. But, at least, the religion of a nation—its creed, its notions concerning supernal natures and invisible things —its views of God and a future life, in short—ought to be such as the noblest and most enlightened Intel-

ligence of the nation can cordially accept and embrace;
and will not either last, or guide, govern, purify, and
elevate the nation if it be not.

Now I allege that in England the highest Intelligence of the nation is not only not in harmony with the
nation's creed, but is distinctly at issue with it; does
not accept it; largely, indeed, repudiates it in the
distinctest manner, or, for peace and prudence's sake,
discountenances it by silence, even where it does not
demur to it in words; and that in this dis-harmony
and divorce lies a grave and undeniable peril for the
future. The fact is not new, but its dimensions are;
the dis-harmony is spreading to many classes, and is
assuming a more pronounced significance; no candid
observer will deny it, and no wise patriot or statesman
will regard it as a matter to be ignored.

The phenomenon in question is neither new in England, nor confined to England; on the contrary, it is
traceable with at least equal distinctness in nearly
every country on the Continent—in France, Spain,
Italy, Belgium, and Germany. In some it has begun
even earlier than here; in some it is yet more marked
and menacing. In France the great outbreak of unbelief at the close of the eighteenth century was, no
doubt, hastened and exasperated by the violent suppression of heresy a hundred years before. The revo-
cation of the Edict of Nantes unquestionably paved
the way to, and largely affected the character of, the
atheistic eruption of the Encyclopædists and the revo-
lutionists three generations later. The Gallican Church,

no doubt, regarded it as a signal triumph when she induced Louis XIV. to silence and banish her comparatively moderate antagonists. "But what was the consequence? Where, after this period, are we to look for her Fenelons and Pascals? where, for those bright monuments of Piety and Learning, which were the glory of her better days? As for piety, she perceived that she had no occasion for it, when there was no lustre of Christian holiness surrounding her; nor for learning, when there were no longer any opponents to confute, or any controversies to maintain. She felt herself at liberty to become as ignorant, as secular, as irreligious as she pleased; and, amid the silence and darkness she had created around her, she drew the curtains and retired to rest." * Acuteness, knowledge, controversial capacity passed over into the hands of her enemies; the Church, long undermined by Voltaire, Rousseau, and their successors, fell with a crash in 1790, and the faith which she had so travestied and dishonoured fell with her: and it is not too much to say, that, since that day—in spite of partial and transient reactions and revivals, of concordats, pilgrimages, galvanic spasms of ghastly activity—nine-tenths of the strongest and finest intellects of France, political, legal, scientific, literary, and polemical, have been arrayed in unconcealed, unceasing, relentless, and contemptuous hostility, not only to the Church and her pretensions, but to every form and claim of Christian-

* Robert Hall, "Modern Infidelity."

ity. Nor is this hostility in any way confined to the intellectual or cultured classes. It prevails in even an exasperated shape among the working men of the whole city population, provincial as well as metropolitan. A really eminent literary or scientific man who should avow himself a Christian would be received with scorn, amazement, or incredulity among his brethren; and an *ouvrier*, who even speaks of religion with respect, becomes suspected by his fellow-toilers from that fact alone. The Divorce of the Intellect of France from her Religion is a *fait accompli;* and how much of her past calamities, and her present chaos and collapse, is traceable to the influence of this divorce, it is impossible to measure.

In Spain, where the amount of intellectual activity and culture is of course far less considerable than in France, whatever there exists is tacitly or avowedly unbelieving, even when not arrayed in actual hostility to the Church. And, indeed, it could scarcely be otherwise, for nowhere probably is Christianity presented in a form so utterly impossible of reception by any trained intelligence; nowhere, too, certainly not in France, are the capacity, the reputation, and the habits of the Priests so little calculated to inspire reverence for the creed they teach, or the pretensions they put forth. The authors of " The Practical Working of the Church in Spain" found the old religion nearly everywhere sinking into contempt. The clergy candidly confessed that they had lost their hold over the middle class; that "if it were not for the

poor there would be no worship of God in the land."
Mr Grant Duff* thus sums up his observations :—

"Our own impression is that the form of Romanism
which prevails in Spain is lower, and retains less of the
real spirit of Christianity than that which exists in any
other Catholic country with which we are acquainted.
Over the lower classes it still has very considerable hold ;
but rather as a superstition than as a religion. On the
other hand, the creed of the bulk of the men among the
educated classes is pure indifferentism, and probably in
their hearts the majority of those who are opposed to religious toleration oppose it in order that they may not have
the trouble of settling what attitude they are to take up
towards the religion of the state. At present they are
Catholics, as a matter of course, just as they are Spaniards.
If they could be anything else, they would be ashamed to
profess belief in a system which they utterly despise. This
state of things need surprise nobody ; it is the natural result of the forcible suppression of free thought, and is seen
in a less degree even in those countries—pagan and other
—where public opinion, and not penal legislation, is the
supporter of the existing creeds. We cannot expect that
miserable hypocrisy, injurious alike to morality, to literature, and to statesmanship, soon to pass away ; but a
beginning is made. Any one who knows Spain could
mention the names of Spaniards who are as enlightened
in these great matters, and as earnest, as the best among
ourselves."

In Germany, where religion presents itself in such
a multitudinous variety of creeds that it might be

---

* "Studies in European Politics," p. 58.

fancied possible for every modification of mind to find
a home in one or other of them, a large majority of
the eminent men in every department of intellectual
enterprise have embraced views which, though by no
means distinctly unbelieving, would certainly not be
recognised as Christian in our country.* And though
it would not be correct to say that in Germany the
Intelligence of the nation is divorced from its Religion, this is solely because the Religion has been so
extensively modified and rationalised by the free
working of the Intelligence, that the natural antagonism which cannot fail to spring up between a progressive culture and a stereotyped and rigid creed which
sternly refuses to accept the slightest innovations (and
which is so manifest and mischievous elsewhere), has
been largely qualified, or altogether evaded.

In Italy the same phenomenon is observable as in
France and Spain, though in a somewhat modified
form and mitigated degree. As in Spain, so in Italy,
Catholicism has long shown itself in forms peculiarly
repellant to cultured and instructed natures, and the
priesthood has been seen too close at hand for its
pretensions to be for a moment tolerated, or its intellectual capacities in the least respected by either
thinkers or observers. But, as in France, the sceptical tendency, inevitable to educated and enlightened

---

* Strauss, in his last work, "The Old Faith and the New,"
answers the question, "Are we still Christians?" for his countrymen, far more distinctly in the negative than I have ventured
to do.

minds, has been complicated and exasperated by
patriotic instincts ; and Religion, embodied in and
therefore confounded with the Church, has presented
itself as the irreconcileable and ruthless foe, not only
of all freedom of thought and intellectual activity or
progress, but of the most passionate aspirations of an
awakened people after national union, liberty, and
greatness. The love of country and the thirst for
truth have therefore in Italy combined to foster deadly
hatred of the common antagonist of both. This may
probably explain a peculiarity which I believe to be
real, but of which I am not informed enough to speak
without diffidence, namely, that whereas in other
Catholic countries the Church has kept its hold upon
the women, in Italy, its connection with local tyranny
and a foreign yoke has united a great proportion of
both sexes in a common detestation.

Finally, we must glance at Belgium, probably far
the most priest-ridden country in Europe. Between
the Catholic Church and Liberal-political institutions
there goes on a fierce and incessant conflict, in which
of late years the Church seems to be gaining ground.
According to M. Emile de Laveleye, the clergy have
nearly made themselves masters of the nation by
means of those very free institutions which they combat and condemn. They are the most unwearied and
successful of electioneerers. The Liberal chiefs, no
longer as a rule believers, are at a grievous disadvantage in the strife, because unprepared openly to avow
their unbelief ; and are discovering too late that, in

order practically to defeat the pretensions of the Church, it is necessary to assail and to renounce its creed.   The following comments of M. de Laveleye on the state of affairs in Belgium are full of warning and suggestion :*—

" How happens it that the liberal party has thus lost ground in a free country, and what means can be used to resist ultramontanism ?   A grave problem, involving the future of catholic countries.   *The weakness of the liberal party comes from the fact of its having to confront a situation full of contradictions.*   Catholicism having, by the mouth of its infallible chief, condemned liberty and modern civilisation, a good and sincere Catholic can no longer defend these liberties.   What can be done by one who would fain save them at all costs ?   Separate himself from the church ?   *But neither people nor family could live without faith.   So the liberal is forced to surrender his wife, his children, and the schools to the priest, whose influence he tries as hard as he can to combat.   On one side he attacks him without cessation, and on the other he invites him, appeals to him, and has daily recourse to his ministration.*   This contradiction is the deeply-seated cause of the weakness of the liberal party.

" To make a way out from this desperate position, an association has been formed with the name of *La libre Pensée*, the members of which undertake to celebrate births, marriages, and burials, without the intervention of the clergy.   This society counts a certain number of adherents, but it is not likely to extend, for not many people will go so far as to renounce publicly all positive religion.   The only course would be to pass over to the reformed catholi-

---

* *Fortnightly Review*, Nov. 1873.

cism of Döllinger and Père Hyacinthe, or else to Protestantism. Since the Church proclaims as a dogma that she and modern civilisation exclude one another, the plain conclusion for those who do not wish to sacrifice liberty is to quit the Church that condemns it. But the time of great religious movements seems gone. The unconscious scepticism of our epoch has so enervated men's souls that they have not enough energy left to abandon a creed in which they have ceased to believe.

"Not long ago it used to be supposed that the political influence of religion was about to disappear. Facts now clearly prove this to have been a mistake. The action of religion on the fortunes of nations is immense and decisive. The constitution of the state ends by modelling itself after that of the church ; or, if not, then the state remains a prey to periodical troubles. Protestantism resting on free inquiry and individual interpretation, the constitutional and representative *régime* is the political form that best suits the reformed nations. Catholics realizing the ideal of an absolutist organization, absolutism is the natural constitution of catholic nations : this is what Bossuet maintained, and he was right. The French revolution, and the men who have adopted its principles, like the Belgian legislators of 1830, thought they found a solution in separating the church from the state. Let the church, they said, govern itself in its own way within its own domain. The state will constitute itself on the base of modern principles within an independent sphere which it will make respected. The attempt has failed, because the clergy will not accept the separation of the church from the state. They mean to rule the state. It is necessary therefore either to submit or fight. The offered truce has been refused. *But to fight against the influence of the church, it is necessary to attack its creed.* This is what the Philosophers of the eighteenth century did.

That was the peculiar task of Voltaireanism. By spreading
Voltairean ideas, you manage to hold ultramontanism in
check. Hitherto, that has succeeded in France, Italy,
Spain, and Portugal. Only this success has cost dear, for
in spreading scepticism you have weakened the moral
spring, and so prepared that confused and morbid state
from which catholic states have so much trouble in emerg-
ing. When we reflect on recent events and on the present
situation of the Continent, we are driven to the conviction
that the solution propounded by the French revolution has
not succeeded. If the country preserves its faith like
Belgium and Ireland, it will fall into the hands of the
clergy. If it forsakes its faith, it will fall into anarchy,
like Spain and Mexico."

Such is the state of affairs in the principal continental countries. The case of England is widely
different. Here the mass of the nation, even of its
educated classes, are still sincere, if not very consistent
or logical, believers. They may not have inquired
deeply or systematically into the foundations of their
faith, but they are attached to it, and do not question
it. Some modify this or that dogma of their creed to
suit their reason, or to bring it into harmony, as they
would say, with the growing enlightenment of the
age. Some discard details which they dimly perceive
or feel to be obsolete. The Christianity of thousands
may be little different from the " civilised heathenism"
it has been named by a popular writer ; the theory
of many and the practice of most may be what divines
would disavow, and what probably Christ would have
been utterly unable to recognize as his teaching ; but

still they call, and would enrol themselves as Christians; they accept the doctrines of their respective
Churches and Sects, and feebly, fitfully, and at a distance, are supposed to guide their conduct by the
precepts of their faith. Not only Religion, but their
special form of it, largely influences their thoughts,
and materially modifies their behaviour. Collectively
the nation recognizes Christianity, feels and enforces
respect for its fancied ordinances and its accredited
administrators, and, when not too difficult or too
inappropriate, follows, or assumes to follow in the
course it preaches. Nay, we may go much farther
than this: the number among us whose temper is
imbued, and whose indifference or selfishness is controlled and transmuted by a genuine Christian spirit,
is so vast, as essentially to modify and colour the
general social aspect of the nation. "The faith of
Jesus," whatever that may mean, is undeniably a
living influence in our community, both upon our
thought and our action. Nevertheless, it is true even
here that the Divorce I have spoken of between the
highest Intelligence of the nation and its Religion—
that is, its ostensible and professed creed—is inchoate,
"looming," visible in the not very remote distance;
proceedings have been instituted before the great
tribunal of ultimate appeal, and a *Rule Nisi* is about
to issue.

I am well aware that this is a rash assertion, and
one in confirmation of which I can only summon each
man's personal observation and inner consciousness to

testify. It is a statement easy to deny, and impossible to prove. First appearances are dead against it. Indifference to religion certainly is not our national characteristic. Our religious controversies and squabbles may be said to be precisely those which are carried on with the greatest acrimony and pertinacity. Divines and their flocks display a ferocity in their love of Truth, which would be refreshing if it were not so disturbing. Theological dogmas, crotchets, passions are, more than any others, the terror and the stumbling-block of statesmen and social reformers. The nation's religion has long stood in the way of the nation's education. Sectarianism is very powerful, and very full of life. The Church is at least as vigorous and aggressive. Perhaps there is more intellectual activity, if not intellect, enlisted in the work of sects and creeds than in any other career except that of money-making. Religion, in one form or another, stimulates and vivifies the daily life of the English people in a remarkable degree. Still, I believe it to be true, that the strongest mental power, the finest thought, the highest intelligence among us, is yearly diverging more and more from Christianity, is discarding all faith in it, assuming towards it not so much a hostile, as an isolated, neutral, almost supercilious, attitude—an attitude which may perhaps best be described as one of silent renunciation and disapproval—of looking, and "passing by on the other side." The preponderant intellect in every line —statesmanlike, legal, scholarly, scientific, literary,

industrial—is no longer *believing*, is, as a rule, distinctly *unbelieving;* and I venture to say this in the
face of such flagrant and splendid contradictions as are
offered by the names of Gladstone, Selborne, Acton,
Faraday, and Wordsworth ; well knowing, also, that
the still greater names I might, if it were not
unseemly, quote in proof of my assertion, would in
many cases not be ready to avow their disbelief, and
in some would resent its being attributed to them.
In a country like England, where conformity to at
least some form of Christianity is enforced by still
extant legal penalties of a very harsh character, and
by social penalties nearly as intolerant and severe, it
is not easy to avow entire dissent from the National
Creed ; and, therefore, the weight and numbers of
such Dissenters will never be accurately known till
they have become preponderant—if, indeed, they ever
should.

I must, therefore, be content to argue on the *assumption*—admittedly unprovable—that this Divorce (and
latent antagonism) between the highest Intellects of
the Nation and the National Belief is in progress and in
view, though by no means as yet an established fact ; *
and that, being in progress, it is a phenomenon ominous of danger.   `

---

* A strong collateral confirmation may be found in the disposition so manifest of late years among the most large-minded of our
Divines, to modify, volatilise, ignore, eliminate, or cover with a
mystical and nebulous halo (as Coleridge did), some of the least
credible features of their creed

Sooner or later the Thinkers of a People must inoculate and inter-penetrate that people with their thought;
and the great thinkers of England are not believers.
The educated classes, as a whole, are still believers;
but the most highly-educated among them have ceased
or are ceasing to be so. The tone of conversation;
the concessions to free speculation that are now habitually admitted; the opinions and doctrines that are
avowable and allowed, and that it would be deemed
intolerance and bad manners to suppress or resent;
and the enormous change that has taken place in
society and in literature, in these respects, in a single
generation, all are indications pointing in the same
direction. The change in the tone of controversial
writing is another; the advocates of established creeds
are no longer assailants, but are content to stand on
the defensive—and cannot always stand. The marked
disinclination which, I am assured, prevails at the
universities among the ablest of the undergraduates to
enter holy orders, may also be referred to as a significant feature.—Another very important fact must also
be adduced. A very large proportion, probably the
majority, of the operative classes in towns are total
unbelievers; and these are not the reckless and disreputable, but, on the contrary, consist of the best of
the skilled workmen, the most instructed and thoughtful, as well as the steadiest. The hard-headed, industrious, reading engineers and foremen, the members of mechanics' institutes, the natural leaders of the
artizans, are sceptics intellectually, not morally; they

disbelieve because they have inquired, argued, and observed, and have been unable to obtain from their Methodist fellow-workmen, or even from ministers of the Gospel, satisfactory answers to their doubts. Among manufacturing artisans and the highest description of citizen labourers, it may be stated, with even more confidence than of the ranks above them in the social scale, that the intellect of the body is already divorced from the prevalent creeds of the country.*

The range and form of this scepticism varies widely in the different classes. Among working men it is for the most part absolute atheism, and is complicated by a marked feeling of antagonism towards the teachers of Religion, a kind of resentment growing out of the conviction that they have been systematically deluded by those who ought to have enlightened them. Thinkers of the higher order among the educated classes, and more especially scientific men, by no means as a rule go so far as this, but content themselves with pronouncing God to be unknowable, and His existence unprovable ; the distinctive doctrines of Christianity, and the details of its historical basis neither made out nor in any way admissible ; and a future life to be a matter of pure speculation, which may or may not be in store for us, but as to which no rational man would dare to dogmatise. Literary men and scholars are often sceptical merely as to special creeds, though

---

* I am assured, however, that this can scarcely be stated as broadly as a few years ago—considerably owing to the Ritualists.

sincerely and deeply religious in tone and temperament. But all concur in repudiating existing forms
of Christianity—that is, the common religion of the
nation ; the Jehovah of the Bible, the Heaven and
the Hell of Divines and Priests, the Resurrection of
the Gospels, and the salvation-formulas of Creeds and
Churches.—We have now to inquire briefly into the
evils menacing our national well-being, which are
likely to spring up from this attitude of mind both in
our highest trained Intellect, and among the most
vigorous and steady of our artizans.

The worst of these evils, so salient in Continental
countries, afflicts us in England, thank God ! only in a
very modified degree. The mental severance observable
there in family life, is far less marked here than either
in France, Italy, or Belgium. Congregations do not
consist very flagrantly of one sex only. The men are
not, as a rule, unbelievers, while the women and children are still orthodox, or at least unsceptical. The
women of the upper and middle classes are not nearly
so much under the influence of the clergy, nor so systematically manipulated by them—neither are the men
so independent or antagonistic—as in Catholic nations
abroad. Here there is a sufficient variety of sects,
and sufficient emancipation from the absolute necessity
of affiliation to any sect, to enable even indifferentists
and sceptics to secure a fair education for their children without having them mischievously inoculated
with doctrines which the parents disapprove. Moreover, religion has not yet assumed that obtrusive and

predominating place in all schools and colleges which it is apt to insist upon where priests are openly at issue with statesmen, and where the Church and its. creeds are fighting for their life; and which there is some danger of its assuming, even in this country, as the conflict, comparatively latent now, becomes more conscious and more critical. There are still seminaries—and (thanks to the strong sense and the imperious will of our unfanatical educated classes) will always be—where first-rate intellectual training can be given to the youth of the nation with no more admixture of dogmatic Christianity than parents may count upon correcting in after life by their own teaching, or eliminating by the slow enlargement and enlightenment of years. Education can be managed without the necessity of either handing over the plastic nature of the child wholly to the Priest on the one hand, or placing it under an avowedly secular system on the other. Still, two serious mischiefs remain, both of them very pernicious to the happiness and integrity of our national life :—in a large, and I fear a growing degree, the perfect openness and confidence which should exist in family life, and without which family life can never reach its ideal point, is impaired; and the brave sincerity which ought to stamp the social intercourse of man with man is dangerously compromised.

The vast numerical majority of both sexes among the educated classes is still believing, but the proportion of sceptics is growing fast; and (which is the

important point whereon to concentrate our attention)
it is growing far faster in one sex than in the other.
The tendency of the masculine intellect is towards inquiry; that of the feminine intellect is towards recep-
tiveness. The one is more logical, the other more
emotional; and as logic strengthens, or where logic
prevails, there, as all experience shows, faith and positive creeds almost unavoidably lose ground. Moreover, what the highest Intelligence of the nation *is*,
the prevalent masculine Intelligence of the nation is
assuredly on the way to become. The day is, therefore, approaching, and in sight, when the mass of cultivated men and cultivated women will no longer think
alike on religious subjects. External conformity may
be preserved often at considerable sacrifice, but that
genuine harmony, which is the secret of inner peace
in " domestic life," will suffer hazardous interruptions
and sad enfeeblement. The mischief will be grave
just in the ratio of the common earnestness. In proportion to the mental integrity of the husband, and
the depth and sincerity of religious feeling in the wife
—in proportion as both parties are conscious that the
topics on which they differ are precisely those in which
difference goes deepest down into the tenderest recesses and the richest springs of the inner life—will
the "fault" (to speak geologically) most jar, will the
jagged edge of the broken link be most painfully and
roughly felt. Woman needs sympathy in all her feelings—most sympathy in those which are most exqui-
site and sacred; if she does not find it at home, she

will seek it abroad—in the church or the vestry, at
the rectory, or at the manse. Confidence and reliance
tend to follow sympathy; the Priest, or the Pastor,
with no blame perhaps on either side, steps into the
husband's chair; and this no Englishman will endure
without bitter pain and a savage struggle. In Catholic
countries often a sort of compassionate and tender
indulgence, which has in it a touch of unacknowledged
scorn, enables the husband to concede religion and
religious exercises and religious consolations to his
wife as something which her frame requires, but which
his manlier nature can dispense with. But this spuri-
ous substitute for blended being lies too far below our
ideal to content us for an hour.

In most instances a further element of bitterness
will follow want of harmony in the religious views, and
will be severest in the most devoted natures. The
mournful and revolting tenet, which is common to
most Sects and Churches, and avowed when they are
rudely pressed, that Salvation depends not on character, but on creed, too often clouds with the most cruel
of anxieties the years of a believing wife linked with
an unbelieving husband; leaves to her restless affection no secure hour of sunshine or effusion over which
the shadow of a nameless terror may not steal;—nay,
as devoted love is usually too vigilant to be judicious,
is apt to make the domestic hearth one long scene and
course of Proselytism, which in the end becomes, or
seems like, Persecution. To be for ever feared for,
prayed for and exhorted, in place of being cherished,

trusted, and believed in, is a trying fate ; and perhaps the sun in his wide circuit shines down upon no sadder spectacle than such strange misuse of Faith and Love when priests' and women's misconceptions of the life that may be are brought in, not to ennoble or embellish, but to embitter and torment the life that is,— and God himself is summoned in to assist in the perversion.

The second mischief indicated may be despatched with very few words. An assumption is tacitly current in society which is the reverse of true, and which taints the whole air of social life with insincerity. The leading minds of the nation are supposed to be believers—and they are not. Nay, more ; not only are they presumed to hold the ordinary views, but it would be deemed uncourteous, if not insulting, to presume otherwise ; and properly so, because to presume, or to speak as if we presumed, otherwise would be, in the current state of narrow intolerance which prevails everywhere but in the great centres of intelligence, to hold them out to the reprobation of the mass of men. In consequence the leading Intellects of whom we speak, partly out of unworthy deference to established prejudice, partly out of mistaken consideration for the weaker brethren, are apt to acquiesce in the tacit assumption of the outer world; and thus timidity is generated among the higher, and impertinence among the commonplace orders of intelligence. The inferior brains impose silence on the superior by virtue of their numbers, and in no field is the tyranny of lower natures so pernicious as in that of mind. The evil is of no modern date; it has been felt more or less in every age of partial and undiffused light; but a mischief is none the less grave for being as old as the time of Socrates.

We must now turn to speculate on the political and social consequences to be anticipated when scepticism shall have spread among the masses of the community; when the doubts and denials of the more cultivated minds shall be no longer concealed from classes wholly unprepared to bear them; when, in a word, the bold unbelief which already prevails among the more trained and strong-headed artisans of our cities, shall have taken possession of the great body of those who live by labour. What changes must we look for, and what dangers shall we run, when the Proletariat as a whole shall have ceased to believe in a God who has ordained their lot and prescribed their conduct, or in a future life which is to redress the inequalities and atone for the often wretchedness of this? The day of this sad apocalypse may be far distant; but in spite of revivals of many sorts and in many quarters, it is difficult to doubt that the current has set in that direction. Now, the first point which it is important to remark in this connection is, that Scepticism takes a different form in comparatively uncultivated and in elaborately educated classes. What is *doubt* in the latter appears as *denial* in the former. The hard, rough, plain, trenchant intelligence of the self-made, self-trained man of the people—accustomed to see

only one side of the shield, to call a spade a spade,
to use clear words to express distinct ideas, to discern
only broad lights, and overlook, ignore, or despise all
shadings and nuances—adopts a very sharp outline
into all his convictions, and holds them with a rigid
positiveness sometimes rather startling to more flexible
and better furnished minds disciplined in the niceties
and subtleties of the schools, aware that language is
but a very imperfect vehicle of thought, especially in
metaphysical and theological matters, and conscious
that there may be often a latent grain or element or
nucleus of undeveloped truth in propositions that,
broadly stated, seem glaring and unmingled falsehood.
The fine, scholastic, matured thinker, like Coleridge,
can say and unsay things in a breath, can almost
affirm and deny propositions in a sentence ; and inferior intellects of the same order can "half say one
thing and half believe another." But the shrewd,
honest mechanic can do nothing of the sort, and has
no great respect or trust for the man who can. His
instrument of thought is not delicate enough to play
with dogmas, and want of downright assertion or
negation appears like want of integrity to him. He
cannot suspend his judgment : with him unbelief
immediately and inevitably becomes disbelief, and
disbelief fast becomes mixed with contempt and
indignation towards the sceptic or the half-believer,
whom he regards as coquetting and tampering with
the unclean thing. Nebulous tenets, vague dissent,
luminous conceptions with a coloured halo round

them, are not for the skilled workman : he is angry
with the Teachers of a Church that has so long
misled him, and seems bent on mystifying him
still. When the lower classes reach the point, therefore of abandoning Christianity, their rejection of it will
be not, as often among the upper ranks, languid and
reserved, but absolute and most probably resentful.
Their disbelief will be apt to be as intolerant and
dogmatic as the credence of the Orthodox.

The operation of unbelief, too, upon minds of this order
will probably be as different as its special intellectual
form. Religion—the precepts and the tenets of the
revealed Word—lie much more distinctly. immediately,
and exclusively at the basis of morality, states of
feeling, and social order, with them than with us.
We can *underpin* these things by the resources of
Philosophy—they cannot. We can see that, even
were the Commandments of Sinai and the Mount of
Galilee discarded, or had they never been, the interests
and the good sense of men would dictate and impose
a course of conduct to each other almost identical
with that which has now the sanction of Christianity.
The Code of duty to ourselves and towards our fellows
would be pretty much the same, though the motives
enforcing it were altogether changed. The theoretical
foundation might be removed and replaced, without
materially affecting the practical superstructure. But
it would scarcely be so with even the best instructed
of the mass of mankind. They have been so trained
to be good and do right, to forego luxury and to

endure hardship, to respect property and control passion, in the name of the Ten Commandments and the Sermon on the Mount, that to be told to do all these things in the name of "a well understood self-interest," and for the benefit of humanity at large, and the development of their own higher natures, would be a startling change of front in the face of an ever-watchful foe—the most notoriously perilous of tactical operations. .It might overset the stability of their entire conceptions of self-rule. The accredited teachers of our population have so habitually held the language: " Be virtuous, because your eternal welfare is at stake upon the issue, and because you shall be repaid ten-fold,"—that they will scarcely be heard or understood when they begin to say instead : " Be virtuous, because you ought, because it is wise to be so. There are, probably, no endless torments for the vicious and malignant, no bliss indescribable through all ages for the unselfish and the pure : there is no Heaven and no Hell, as you were once taught ; but the bosom of the bad man is a Hell of stormy passions, and the bosom of the righteous is a Heaven of sunshine and of peace. We lay upon you the same obligation of ceaseless self-control and self-denial as before ; but the objective, concrete, intelligible, *sure* recompense for a life of effort and of patience which we could once so confidently promise must no longer be a portion of your creed. The burden of duty remains as heavy as ever, but you may no longer count upon the old ample wages at the close of the weary day."

There can, I think, be little question that the doctrine of Christianity which has exercised the widest influence—the widest *police* influence, so to speak, though perhaps not the most wholesome moral influence, has been its delineation of the future life as one of *compensation* for the troubles and inequalities of this. The teaching of the Gospel is startlingly explicit on this head. The last are to be first ; the poor are to be rich ; the slave is to be free ; those who had a bad time of it here are to have a good time of it there—and *vice versâ*. The doctrine has been ridden hard ; it has had much to do, and has done it well. " This light affliction, *which is but for a moment*," is to be repaid by an exceeding, even an eternal recompense. The joys and pains of earth are so poor and so short in comparison with those of the next world, that those who have drawn blanks in the lottery of life below ought to esteem themselves in truth the favoured of fortune, and would be foolish as well as rebellious to murmur or to envy. This sublunary scene is only the first act of the drama : the last act will set all right—will reverse as well as rectify the balance. No doctrine could have been devised so admirably qualified to instil endurance and content amid the privations and inequalities of human lots, to make the needy, the suffering, and even the oppressed, patient under what they have almost been induced to regard as a passing cloud or an insignificant distinction. No bolts or bars, no laws, no army of retainers, have been such effective guardians of the possessions

of the great and affluent; the established order of
things has had no defence half so cheap, half so mighty,
or of half such unsleeping vigilance. Why, indeed,
should men of sense seek to overthrow arrangements
and distributions of the elements of happiness that the
brief space of fifty years will reverse for ever in their
favour ?   I am far from saying that the doctrine is
unassailable ; still less that it has operated on the
whole beneficially on the material progress of mankind;
I am only pointing out what a potent ally it has been
to the governing, enjoying, richly endowed classes of
the earth.   What will be the result, what the possible
catastrophe, when this doctrine is no longer accredited—
when it is discarded as a delusion—when it is resented
as a convenient deception and instrument of oppression ; when the poor man is convinced that there is no
wealth of gold and jewels awaiting him in the spiritual
kingdom—that if he is wretched here, he is wretched
altogether—that what he lacks now will never hereafter be made good to him—that the promises and
hopes dangled before him to keep him quiet have been
mere moonshine, and that in very truth the bank in
which he had insured his fortune, in which he had
invested all his savings, to have a provision in which
he had toiled with indefatigable industry and endured
with exemplary patience, is a fraudulent insolvent;
when, in fine, he wakes up with a start to the be-
wildering conviction that *if* he is to rest, to be happy,
to enjoy his fair share of the sunshine and the warmth
of life, *he must do it now, here, at once, without a*

day's delay ? Will there not come upon him that sort
of feverish haste to be in luxury and at peace, to *im-
mediatize* all that earth can yield him, to sink the
uncertain future in the passing present, which has
been depicted in such vivid colours as pervading and
maddening the daily thought and talk of the Socialists
and Communists of the French metropolis ? If his
paradise is to be here or nowhere, why should there
be a moment lost in beginning to construct it ? and
why, again, should any other man's wealth or welfare
stand in his way ? If he is not to have the upper-
hand elsewhere, why should he submit to be kept
under now ? Will there not come upon him, also, the
ominous question—a question to which in his ignorance and his passion he will have no answer ready—
" Why should not I, whose time is so short, *take* what
it will need so many slow hard years to win ?" And
with all this will there not come—there did come in
Paris—a fierce resentment at the flagrant inequalities
around him, the comparative (often positive) wretchedness in which he has hitherto remained, and the fables
which he has been told to pacify him,—till he will
hate as well as envy those above him, and learn to
regard their spoliation as an act of righteous restitution ?

It may be maintained with considerable plausibility
that the purely *arbitrary* inequalities of men's lots
and fortunes are by no means as vast or as habitual
as at first appears ; that those who are indigent and
wretched without fault of their own or their parents,

are in most communities comparatively few ; that, if
the poor were as prudent, as sagacious, and as energetic as the well-to-do, or the well-to-do as unthrifty
and improvident as the poor, the individuals of the
respective classes would often change places ; and that
in a well-ordered and decently educated nation there
would seldom be discrepancies of earthly condition
obviously and distinctly needing a future world, regu-
lated on altogether different principles, to redress the
unmerited balance of the present.   It may be argued,
too, with much more than plausibility, that, be there
a reversing and compensatory hereafter, or be there not,
the variations and injustices of men's earthly conditions cannot be rectified by class spoliations and up-
risings, or by social revolutions ; that masses of men
cannot become affluent or happy by a leap; that the
only road to competence and leisure is the old one,
and the only reliable instruments those which have
wrought successfully in all ages—industry, frugality,
persistence, and instruction.   But it demands mental
and moral enlightenment of no common order for the
unfortunate and destitute, living in the midst of luxury
and splendour, to recognise the absolute accuracy of
of these " wise saws" and sober economic reasonings ;
and the ignorant, undisciplined, and reckless may
fairly enough plead that the very lack of intelligence
and self-control which has made and kept them squalid
and miserable is itself almost as much a cruel partiality of fortune as the lack of land or funds.   It may
well be that if the pedigree of wealth and wisdom, of

privation and ignorance, of health and disease, were traced far enough back and with omniscient insight, some points and personages in the ancestry of each would afford at once the explanation and the justification of the painfully unequal apportionment we see, and so "vindicate the ways of God to man." But no one, except a born philosopher, will ever recognize with cordial acceptance, the absolute equity of the decree which makes him suffer for his father's and forefathers' incapacities or errors; the actual inequalities of men's lot, both as to enjoyments, opportunities, and possessions, are so utterly enormous in nearly every civilized country, and so admittedly excessive and undesirable; to him that hath is so habitually given, and from him that hath not is so ruthlessly taken away the little he hath; so many spend their lives among struggles and pains which, if this life be all, are at once inexplicable and unspeakably grievous, that only the prospect of a far different and absolutely certain future can ever heartily *reconcile* the less lucky among us to the sights we see around us. And if mere observers feel this, how incomparably more vivid must be the sentiments of the sufferers !

No doubt the practical, if grumbling, acquiescence in the prevalent inequalities of fortune, and in the privations and hardships of their own condition, which is the normal state of the masses in most European and in nearly all Asiatic countries, is due, not exclusively to their religious hopes, but in a very large, though varying measure, to two other influences—

K

namely, the actual or potential repressive force of police and law, and the unconscious but leaden, almost mountainous weight of habit. The social system, with its imposing hierarchy, its half-invisible but time-honoured fences, its grey old massive walls, its thousand buttresses and bulwarks and interlacing of *chevaux-de-frise*, lies upon the mind of the peasant, the citizen, the artizan who for generations has grown up amidst it, with a solid pressure which is only disturbed by crises of unusual fermentation. His thoughts are moulded by it, as those of his ancestors have been; what has been so long seems to him almost as if it was there by a law of nature; what stands so firmly looks as if it stood by right; what *is* conveys the impression that it ought to be. This invaluable legacy from the past, this inherited stability, is a mighty power in support of the existing order of things, but it operates only, or mainly, while unquestioned; let rude inquiry, pert denial, insinuating doubt, pertinacious demand for the production of title-deeds, once come into the field, and the spell is broken. Its magic may not be dispelled at once—there is strange tenacity of life in such hereditary sentiments; but the foundations are undermined by degrees; and some leaves fall off every time the tree is shaken. Now, in most countries, certainly in England, every existing social institution, every origin and sustenance of our unequal distribution of this world's goods, has been put on its defence, and it is hard to deny that weak places have been found; Communistic theories have been much discussed, and discussed in circles where the flimsiest arguments are not easily distinguished from the most cogent; and even cultivated intellects and keen economists have not been wanting to maintain that the actual distribution of property and opportunities is unwarrantable and unfair. The official guardians of rank, property, and order—Administration, Soldiers, and Policemen — are still upright, and present a formidable and to all appearance an irresistible array, and the classes who have are as yet far stronger than those who want; but the latter are the more numerous, and the two are curiously intermingled. The masses, too, have still a wholesome and well-founded conviction that in case of violence or attempted spoliation their numbers would be almost powerless against the solid front of law and its authorized executors. But nevertheless the conclusion remains and admits of no dispute,—and it is on this that I wish to concentrate the attention of my readers :—that, when the change I have indicated shall have come over the religious belief of the working classes in this country, the burden of protecting our anomalous and unequal system and of maintaining the Social Hierarchy as it now exists—hitherto sustained by the belief in a compensating world hereafter, by the force of ancestral sentiment and habit, *and* by the armed force of Government and Law, *i.e.*, by the three in combination—will be thrown upon the two last powers exclusively ;—that one of those at least is already materially weakened, and that the other (as I showed in my first paper) has been deliberately under-mined.

When we look · around in search of agencies by which the evil I have indicated may be mitigated or averted, we see three—effectual enough, perhaps, if put in operation, but the adoption of which can scarcely be anticipated with very sanguine confidence. Perhaps they all—two of them certainly—partake too much of the old infantine recipe for catching birds by putting salt upon their tails.

A teaching at once economic and philosophical, which should embue the minds of the people with the conviction (undoubtedly, we apprehend, the true one) that, as a rule, the course of action of the wise and good man will be the same on earth, whether there be a further scene of existence or not, would neutralise the most obvious and the coarsest of the dangers to which the abjuration of the Christian creed must otherwise expose the country. The prac-tical maxims for the conduct of life, which would be laid down by a moralist and lawgiver thinking only of the happiness of the individual and the wellbeing of society, would not be so widely different from the precepts of the gospel, modified and interpreted as those now are by the requirements of our actual civilisation and the tem-peraments of modern thought, as to cause any sudden disruption or confusion when the basis of allegiance and sanction was transferred. The ethical and legal codes would remain substantially the same, though the authority which framed them and the ruler who enforced them had been changed. Whether the goal at which we aim be an ideal heaven, or a worthy earth and a perfected humanity—whether the penalties we seek to avoid be those of a scriptural hell or of human reprobation and social inflictions — the majority of the actions to be wrought or eschewed would probably not be as discrepant as we might at first imagine; for the lessons of enlightened self-interest, if not exactly generous or ennobling, are apt with trained intellects to be very efficient ; and the affections, after all, are the most potent influences to action among believers and unbelievers alike. A moral Governor of the universe, and a thoroughly sagacious Ruler of the community would lay down much the same principles of action, though the tone of the former would be loftier, his requirements severer, and his language more positive than negative —dealing rather with commands than prohibitions. No doubt, with the loss of a God who sees our doings, and who rewards obedience with absolute fidelity, much of the buoyant cheerfulness of virtue might die out ; still, on the whole, it would have to be admitted that, even without a God, duty persistent and enlightened pays at last. No doubt, with no hope of a coming world of rest, of compensation, and of undying felicity, the brightest colours would fade out of life, and a sadder, soberer hue would steal over the prospects of humanity. Still, if men were what they ought to be and might be, Earth, we all trust, might grow immeasurably nearer to a Heaven than it is. We

should not be surrendering, or ceasing to aim at an
ideal Future; but that future would be less distant and less dim; it would be located nearer to us;
it would be more scientifically wrought for; its constituent elements would be such as the mass of men
could better appreciate and realise.   Nay, it has been
argued,* and it is difficult to refute the argument,
that the prevalent doctrine of a future life, in the
hands of the Church, has often exercised an influence
by no means friendly on the material wellbeing of
communities—an influence which has gone far to
neutralise its beneficial operation in an ethical direction.

But unfortunately for the prospect of such philosophic views as I have suggested being adopted as a
basis for the practical moral code to be henceforth
inculcated in our community, the habitual language
of the majority of Christian teachers has pointed in a
diametrically opposite direction.   They have spoken
as if, apart from a future life, the law of self-sacrifice
could have no significance or obligation,—as if laying
down life and joy for Love's, or Truth's, or Virtue's
sake, would be mere folly, if there were no coming
scene where such surrender would be instantly recom-
pensed tenfold—as if even self-denial, self-control, the
postponement of an immediate to a distant good—of
a lower to a nobler aim—were almost questionable
sense.   They have often even sunk below the stan-

---

* "Enigmas of Life," Realisable Ideals, pp. 19-26.

dard of Pagan and Prophetic moralists, and preached as if Righteousness was to be followed mainly, if not solely, for the loaves and fishes that would follow it at last—mainly because the payment for it, if not prompt, was at least absolutely certain."* The gospel, indeed, tells us that " Godliness has the promise of the life that now is, as well as of that which is to come :" but this has never been a favourite text among divines, and so complete and rapid a change of front, as our needs may require, is scarcely to be expected from them.

A second source of safety may be found—and, if we are sagacious and forecasting, will be diligently sought—in a prompt rectification of those extremer and crueller contrasts of men's lots on earth for which (if there be no redressing future) Providence might, with at least some show of justice, be arraigned, Nine-tenths of the accusations and reproaches which man flings upon his Maker are monstrously unfair : both because no law of equity even suggests that every human being is entitled to be *as* well-endowed or *as* happy as his neighbour, and because in the majority of instances privations and distresses are

---

* Robert Hall, perhaps the finest and purest genius among them, goes so far as to maintain ("Modern Infidelity," p. 20) that, apart from the hope of future recompense, "a deviation from rectitude would become the part of wisdom ; and should the path of virtue be obstructed by disgrace, torment, or death, to 'persevere would' be madness and folly."

due to his own folly, or are the direct results of a system of causation which in its habitual operation is beneficent as well as righteous. But this thesis cannot be maintained in all cases, nor made convincing to most minds. He would be a bold disputant who should undertake to prove that every man has what he deserves, or ought to be content with what he has ; and even were his argument logically tenable, it is certain that no miscellaneous audience could be made to listen to it with either patience or profit. Disease, pain, and all the life-long wretchedness of incapacitation, are entailed upon the child by parental or ancestral wrong; and the child may recognize in the arrangement an inevitable fate against which it would be idle to rebel, but never a just decree to which it was a duty unmurmuringly to submit. A man may perceive that his destitution is traceable to his ignorance or stupidity, or want of steady purpose and severe self-control; but the very capacity of thought which thus quickens his perception will carry him a step further, and teach him to ask whence came that want of training which lost him all golden opportunities, and left his faculties so undeveloped and so torpid ;—especially when he sees by his side others, originally no whit better than himself, whom advantages and aids, denied to him, have landed in a widely different condition. Refine as audaciously and as ingeniously as we please, the salient fact stares us in the face, that man's share of happiness in our complicated civilization depends more on luck than on merit (if we look deep enough and far back enough into causation), and most of all, perhaps, upon the place and grade in which we first set foot upon this earth. Some open their eyes upon ease and luxury, others upon squalor and privation; the steps of some are surrounded from infancy with the most vigilant care and guidance, the steps of others with habitual neglect; some come into the world saddled and bridled, some booted and spurred;—and on the whole the bright, smooth, joyous life is the portion of the few, and the hard and struggling career is the portion of the many.

Probably no statesmanship and no philanthropy can altogether alter this;—perhaps, even, such narrow statesmanship and such blundering philanthropy as we possess, in attempting to mend matters, may aggravate the mischief. But at least we may remedy those more flagrant discrepancies which no logic can defend and no sophistries can gild; at least we may remove all purely artificial injustice; at least we may abstain from exasperating all natural sufferings and sores. We cannot re-distribute property, but we may see to it that no unwise or partial laws favour unequal distribution. We may so arrange matters that *opportunities* of bettering themselves shall come some time in their life to all; that want of instruction at least shall not hold them back; that industry shall have a fair field, and frugal economy shall find safe investments. We cannot preclude sickness and disease from invading the hovel, where they are so incomparable more disastrous than in the mansion or the palace; but we can at least contrive that they shall not be unavoidable inmates or companions, and that when they come they shall be met by something of the same alleviations and antagonists as among ourselves. In a word, we can and we ought, and if we are wise we shall, without delay proceed so to set our house in order that inequalities shall lose the irritating aspect of injustice; that there should not be the enormous temptation, which there now undeniably is on every side to undisciplined natures deprived of the opiate hopes of a rich hereafter, to covet and seize the alluring treasures which lie so lavishly around them here ; and that every man should be so justly treated, so tenderly cared for, and so sedulously taught, that these two things shall be made very clear to him: —*first*, that competence and comfort lie within his reach by the legitimate path of prudence, integrity, and toil ; and *secondly*, that by no other means and no shorter cut can they ever be secured. I believe it to be possible—I do not say easy—to render property and order respected and secure, even without the aid of a future life, if only our people are intelligent, and our laws are just.

Is there no other way of escape ? Is it hopeless to avert and preclude the danger, instead of meeting and mitigating it when it comes ? Is it idle to dream that in the course of years the religion of the nation may be modified in the direction and under the guidance of its best Intelligence, since that Intelligence can no longer accept the common Creed ?—The thing is possible, but not likely. I seem to see how it might be done, but I have no hope that it will be done. The divergence is too wide ; the sources of the alienation lie too deep. At first sight it would appear as if the essential teachings of Christianity consisted so much of sound morality, pious emotion, and ennobling sentiment which Philosophy would cordially welcome, and of hopes and doctrines which Science, though not affirming or endorsing, makes no pretensions to deny,—that not only peace, but a sincere alliance, might well exist between forms of thought which only misunderstanding and mismanagement have rendered hostile. In the Christian spirit and the basis of the Christian precepts and the kind of character they foster, our highest wisdom finds everything to admire, and nothing to gainsay;— and as regards the belief in a Creator and Moral Ruler of the Universe, and in a future world of retribution and of progress, the scientific Intellect at most is silent and declines to dogmatise. Here, then, one might fancy, is a common ground on which the Religious and the Philosophic mind might meet in friendship, and issue forth to make joint war against the powers of Evil. But unfortunately Theologians have decreed that the vital essence of the Christian Faith shall lie in its other tenets—in historical assertions which Research will not admit—in formulas and " schemes " of Salvation which Reason utterly disputes.

Doubtless there are Divines who take a larger view,
who would willingly keep in the background those
special dogmas which are most open to question and
most liable to distortion and abuse, and whose truer
sense of relative values and proportions would classify
. differently the articles of their Creed ;—and if these
Divines were uppermost or most numerous, and could
give the tone and direction to the Thought of Chris-
tendom, there would be a chance for the reconciliation
which I suggest.   A course of authoritative preaching
from ten thousand pulpits, persistent for an entire
generation, which, without controversy or ostentatious
neglect, should allow Original Sin and Imputed
Righteousness, the legend of the Fall and the story of
the Incarnation, Baptismal Regeneration, Eternal
punishments, the Trinity and the Atonement, gently
to fall into the shade as mysteries which it is vain to
seek to penetrate, and regarding which silence is our
least injurious and most respectful course ;—while the
same preaching should bring out into prominence and
light the doctrines on which Christ most loved to
dwell—the Fatherhood of God, His Omnipresence and
his Love, the conviction that His eye is ever on us,
and his ear ever open to our pleading, the need of
purity and truth in our own nature, and of boundless
sympathy and love to our fellow-men, Jesus as our
pattern and our guide, and the Creator and Guardian
of all as so just, so loving, and so wise, that—doing
his will—we may leave our future in his hands with
absolute trust, insisting on no pledge, prying into no

details, asking for no chart or picture of the vague unknown;—a course of preaching such as this (is it quite in vain to dream ?) might leave our grand-children in possession of a creed wherein every thing that to us is hard, questionable, and repellant, shall have become simply obsolete—a Faith which Piety and Science might combine to uphold—a National Altar before which the highest Intelligence and the most fervent Devotion might in transparent sincerity kneel side by side,—a Religion in which should lurk no seed for wars, no standing-ground for the Sacer-dotal element, no fair pretexts or gorgeous disguises for the low bad passions of humanity.

APPENDIX.

APPENDIX A.

THE MISTAKE OF HONEST DEMOCRATS.

THERE are two theories of what Government should be, springing from entirely distinct foundations, both logical in their way, argumentatively tenable, and capable of being maintained by sensible men with sincere conviction. The one is based upon the doctrine that rule ought to be in the hands of the wise and educated, the mentally, morally, and socially *élite* of the nation, since the mass of the people can never be sufficiently enlightened or instructed to be quali fied judges either of ends or means in political questions. This is the aristocratic or autocratic theory ; it prevailed everywhere in the earliest times, and was then probably unassailable both in premisses and conclusion, and may perhaps, as a mere abstract thesis, be accepted as virtually sound in all times. The other assumes that, as the great body of the citizens of a community advance in civilization, the day comes when they are sufficiently qualified, partly by training and partly by instinct, to govern themselves, or at least to determine how and by whom they will be governed ; when, in fact, though not as well educated or perhaps as wise and able as kings, nobles, and wealthy men of leisure, their greater singleness of view towards their own interests, and closer perception of them, more than com- pensate for their inferior intellectual training and capacity ; and when, therefore, the majority of the people may safely be entrusted with and have a right to claim the reins of power. This is the democratic theory ; and men of

L

"advanced opinions" believe that the day for its application to public matters, in most western countries at least, has already come.

The weak point in the aristocratic theory is that it is very difficult, on any hereditary or autocratic system, to secure that it shall be the wisest, best, most capable who, do govern ; that we shall get the right men to the head of affairs ; or that, when there, we shall be able to rely upon their ruling for the interests of the country at large, and not for their own special behoof. So clearly has this been seen, and so fully has it been exemplified, that the theory itself has fallen into discredit, and is generally discarded among progressive nations. The analogous weak place in the rival doctrine—equally undeniable, equally fatal, perhaps equally incurable—if it has not quite escaped detection, has at least not hitherto been adequately signalized or often recognised. The *theory* affirms, that when a nation has reached a certain stage of advance and education, the majority of the people are competent to govern, or to determine the form and direction and to choose the instruments of government ; and that, being the majority, they ought to have their own way. The *fact* is, that in no democracy *does* the majority of citizens thus choose or govern, any more than in an aristocracy ; that often the more democratic the form of constitution the less are choice and rule really and truly in the hands of the majority ; and that, if this be so, the very basis and main premiss at the root of the democratic theory breaks down.

And is it not so ? Must not the whole practical machinery of modern political action be widely altered before it ceases to be so ? And when it shall have ceased to be so, will not the character and condition of a people have become so disciplined and advanced that almost any rule will be easy and suitable ? The plain truth is, that *democracies*, just like aristocracies — perhaps more than aristocracies—*have a perpetual, nearly irresistible, tendency to degenerate into oligarchies.* Politics, though an exciting, is a troublesome and a busy game, and requires devotion, experience, trained skill. The *many*, in every state, are too poor and too hard-worked to do more than rush into it occasionally ; the few are always at it. The few, therefore, the active politicians, the professional electioneers, get the matter speedily into their own hands, speak for the masses and tell them how to speak; think for them, lead them and mislead them ; organize their action, direct their votes. It must always be so, and it would seem as if it must be more and more so just in proportion to the width of the democratic basis. Even in the most popular and primitive cantons in the east of Switzerland, where the whole body of inhabitants meet in the open air to vote their laws and to elect their magistrates, it is always an active few, a " caucus " in fact, who prepare the resolutions, canvass, and instruct or persuade the electors, propose the candidates—do the work, in short. In our own Trades' Unions, how rarely do the masses of workmen exercise any influence, form or uphold any opinion, decide any important matter ! There is too little individual thought or volition among them, and that little is rarely courageous, is never organized, and, therefore, is always feeble and inoperative. They vote as they are bid, and strike when they are told. They follow others, thinking they are going with the majority, when in truth often half that majority are ignorant or reluctant, and are merely obeying, probably unconsciously, the impulse given them by a small, often unwise, sometimes selfish and dishonest clique. There is, perhaps, no such thorough oligarchy as that often to be found among trades' unions. In America, the land of democracy *par excellence*, whose democracy is possibly more real than elsewhere, because the level of instruction, capacity, and means among the people is more uniform—in the Union as in States, in Congress as in local assemblies, in national as in municipal politics, the management of affairs has fallen into the hands of a regular and a notoriously low profession, of men who make a business of mal-administration, of perhaps the most recklessly dishonest oligarchs on earth:—legislation, as well as elections, is *contracted for.* The nation among nations, with probably the greatest future before it if not great yet, has suffered its politics to be governed and coloured by a small and disreputable minority, and only on very grave occasions, when serious danger is imminent, and after infinite mischief has been done, does the real sound-hearted, rational majority of the people—the shareholders, as it were, among the infamous directors—step in to veto the final folly, and send the daily, ordinary, standing rascals to the right-about. The facts are notorious and deplorable ; and the most graphic illustration of the state of things is presented when vigilance committees, representing the pre-occupied, busy, *poco-curante,* respectable *majority,* have to be organised to sweep away or lynch the judges, sheriffs, police officers, who have been nominated by a lot of harpies and malefactors in the name of the abstinent and passively conniving masses.

Something of the same sort, though very modified and possibly very distant, looms before us in England. The larger the constituencies, the more necessary will committees and experienced electioneerers be found to organise and wield them. The more ignorant they are, the more certain they are to listen to and obey the few who will take the trouble to influence and get hold of " what they are pleased to call their minds." The wider the democracy, the more need of organisation. The whole course of history shows us the superior efficiency—*i.e.,* the superior real power—of an organised and active few over an unorganised and inactive many. The mass have an interest in peace ; but the few find a vast profit to their purses or a sweet comfort to their passions in war ; and as the few rule unless the mass rouses itself, or *till* it rouses itself, (which is usually too late,) war comes upon a nation unwilling and unawares. The majority has an interest in economy ; but the interest of the few in expenditure is so incomparably more intense and vivid because more concentrated, that democracies are proverbially spendthrift. Now, the reason why the few— an oligarchy properly so called, and an oligarchy often of the worst kind—are more sure to bear sway in a democracy than in a State where the nobles or the educated classes predominate, is this :—That in the latter cases a far larger proportion of the real citizens take an interest and are qualified to take a part in politics ; that, being more instructed and enlightened, the interest they take is *more continuous ;* and that, being more independent in mind, their individual volition is far more courageous and influential. *Democracy,* therefore, in nine cases out of ten— and this is the truth we are desirous to impress—*is not the rule of the majority of the people,* but is, *first,* the rule of a smaller number in proportion to that majority ; and, *secondly,* is likely to be the rule of a positively inferior order of intelligence and public virtue, than in States where the basis of citizenship is less extended.

APPENDIX B.

UNIONIST RESTRICTIONS ON LABOUR.

(From Mr Thornton's book on "Labour." Second Edition.
Pp. 344-354.)

"THERE are other unionist proceedings which, only by being enumerated, are almost sufficiently condemned. Some unions divide the country round them into districts, and will not permit the products of the trades controlled by them to be used, except within the district in which they have been fabricated. In most parts of Lancashire the brickmakers and bricklayers' associations are in alliance, offensive and defensive, one consequence of which is that within certain arbitrarily fixed limits, no bricks can be laid that have not been made within the same limits. At Manchester this combination is particularly effective, preventing any bricks made beyond a radius of four miles from entering the city. To enforce the exclusion, paid agents are employed; every cart of bricks coming towards Manchester is watched, and if the contents be found to have come from without the prescribed boundary, the bricklayers at once refuse to work. Four miles from Manchester, and two from Ashton-under-Lyne, runs a canal which the Manchester brickmakers have thought fit to take as their boundary line. On the Ashton bank of this canal lies, unfortunately for its owners, an extensive brickyard; and there, a few months since, 500,000 bricks, besides £300 worth of plant, were remaining as so much dead capital, because in the Ashton townships no building was going on, and because an embargo was in force against the passage of bricks across the canal. The vagaries of the Lancashire brickmakers are fairly paralleled by the masons of the same county. Stone, when freshly quarried, is softer, and can be more easily cut than later : men habitually employed about any particular quarry better understand the working of its particular stone than men from a distance : there is great economy, too, in transporting stone dressed instead of in rough blocks. The Manchester masons, however, will not allow Yorkshire stone to be brought into their district if worked on more than one side. All the rest of the working, the edging and jointing, they insist on doing themselves, though they thereby add thirty-five per cent. to its price. A Bradford contractor, requiring for a staircase some steps of hard Delphstone, a material which Bradford masons so much dislike that they often refuse employment rather than undertake it, got the steps worked at the quarry. But when they arrived ready for setting, his masons insisted on their being worked over again, at an expense of from 5s. to 10s. per step. A master mason at Ashton obtained some stone ready polished from a quarry near Macclesfield. His men, however, in obedience to the rules of their club, refused to fix it until the polished part had been defaced, and they had polished it again by hand, though not so well as at first. Two winters ago a builder at Heywood, willing to keep his men employed during the bad weather and short days, when otherwise there would be little for them to do, allowed them to work up a quantity of stone to be ready for use in the spring. When spring came, however, the very men who had worked the stone, struck work on account of its going off to be fixed at other places. A church was being built at Barrow-in-Furness, for which some moulded limestone bases or plinths were required. At first it was intended to have the stone for these brought from the quarries to Barrow and worked up there, but as the Barrow masons had not got the proper tools for that particular limestone, and as they might reasonably object to having to buy them for only a few days' use, the contractor finally resolved to have the stone sent to his own yard in Liverpool, to be made into bases there by members of the Operative Masons' Society, who are paid at a higher rate than the Barrow members. This was done, and the bases came to Barrow, and were fixed upon the walls ; but immediately afterwards the Barrow lodge, discovering that one of their local rules had been infringed by the importation of worked stone into Barrow, demanded first, that the bases should be worked over again ; secondly, when this was refused as an impossible interference with the architect's design, that as much time as would have been required to re-work them should be occupied by the Barrow masons in standing over them. Finally, the matter was compromised by the contractor's consenting to let the bases be taken from their beds and refused, and promising not to introduce any dressed stone into Barrow again. Much in the same spirit, though somewhat different in form, is another piece of Lancashire practice. According to a rule laid down by the operative bricklayers, whenever a town master undertakes work away from the town he inhabits, one-half of the men employed on the work must belong to that town, and if an uneven number be employed, so must the odd man also. In deference to this rule, an unfortunate Manchester master, who had got an order for the Bury Railway Station at a time when the building trade was brisk at Manchester, did everything in his power to get Manchester men for the job, applying for them, among other quarters, to the union ; but everywhere without success. Then fancying that, in such peculiar circumstances, he might venture to treat exclusively with Bury men, he engaged eleven of these, taking good care that they should be society men ; but scarcely had he set them to work than two of the society's delegates came down upon him from Manchester, bidding him discharge six of the eleven and replace them with Manchester men, or, if he could get none of the latter, then to stop the work till he could ; concluding by asking for their own day's wages, amounting to 7s. each, and 3s. each for first-class railway fare from Manchester, for coming to give him what they called their " orders." The upshot of the affair was that the master did as he was bid in every particular, and had to take men from his other jobs in Manchester to work in Bury, although at the time a large number of bricklayers were out of work in Bury and its neighbourhood.

Some unions, from the minuteness and rigour with which they insist on the division of labour, would almost seem to be bent on establishing among English workmen the obsolete slavery of Hindoo or Egyptian caste. The following examples will show how far they sometimes go in that direction :—

In one or two of the northern counties, the associated plasterers and associated plasterers' labourers have come to an understanding, according to which the latter are to abstain from all plasterers' work, except simple whitewashing ; and plasterers in return are to do nothing, except pure plasterers' work, that the labourers would like to do for them, insomuch that if a plasterer wants laths or plaster to go on with, he must not go and fetch them himself, but must send a labourer for them. In consequence of this agreement, a Mr Booth of Bolton, having sent one of his plasterers to bed and point a dozen windows, had to place a labourer with him during the whole of the four days he was engaged on the job, though anybody could have brought him all he required in half a day. It appears to be usual in some places for the same persons to be brought up as plasterers and bricklayers, learning both trades together. A Scarborough builder, however, who had given his bricklayers some plastering to do, after they had finished their bricklaying, got notice from the Plasterers' Union, that if he let the bricklayers proceed, he would have to finish with them, for that no regular plasterers should in that case be permitted to serve him. One of the adepts at both trades, who, from having been in business on his own account, was reduced to go out as a journeyman, got employment as a plasterer from a master who had known him in better days. The other plasterers, however, would not let him stay: as he professed to be as much a bricklayer as a plasterer, he should not, they said, work as a plasterer; he might go somewhere else, and work as a bricklayer. In vain the poor fellow pleaded the wife and large family dependent upon him for bread. His persecutors were obdurate, and left his and their employer no alternative but to part either with him or with them.

At Bolton, some bricklayers passing by a Mr Day's place of business, and hearing some hammering of brickwork going on within, looked inside and saw a carpenter who had been sent to fix some joists, enlarging the holes which had been left in the brickwork for the joists. For suffering the carpenter to do this, the bricklayers fined Mr Day £2. At Ashton-under-Lyne, Mr George Colbeck sent a joiner and a bricklayer to make some alterations in a house, the door of which was to be removed half the width of itself. The bricklayer built up the part requiring it; but because the joiner, instead of standing idly by while this was being done, presumed to pull out some few bricks that had to be removed, the bricklayer struck work and left the job. Colbeck in consequence was fined £2 by the Bricklayers' Union. He naturally asked what for? The reply was, that he had infringed rules by permitting a joiner to pull out bricks, which ought to be done by a bricklayer, and that all the jobs on which he was engaged should be

stopped ; so he paid. At another place a builder was fined
£5. His offence was that, after waiting five days for a bit
of brickwork—the widening of one window opening—which
he could not get his bricklayers to do, because they were
away on a prolonged drinking bout, he at last in despair
got a mason to do it. These are bricklayers' feats, but
there is nothing they do which masons cannot cap. Some
of both were employed together in restoring the old church
at Kenilworth, of which part of the old stonework had to
be cleaned down, and the joints raked out and pointed.
This is work which, in that part of the country, bricklayers
are specially qualified for, and which masons do not understand. No sooner, however, were two of the former set
upon it, than all the latter struck, although on being questioned, they were obliged to admit that there was not one
amongst them who could do the work at all. In the neighbourhood of Sheffield, two bricklayers had been sent to
" tuck-point " a wall ; but when they had been at it for
a week, their master was compelled to withdraw them because his masons threatened to strike if he did not. The
masons were then asked whether they could do the work,
and one and all replied that they could not, some adding
that they would not if they could, for that they would be
obliged to get new tools for it, such as they had never used
before. Still they would let no one else do it, and the wall
in consequence remained unfinished for months. If members of the painting craft, less frequently than their masonic
cousins, resent foreign interference, it can only be for want
of opportunity. That the spirit of exclusiveness is as strong
in them as in any other building operatives, will be made
manifest by one single example. The book-keeper of a
house-painting firm at Blackpool wanting to measure up
some work, and finding the marks on his measuring-rod
nearly obliterated, took up a little paint, and painted the

inches and feet upon it afresh; whereupon his employers
got a letter from theirs "respectfully, the committee, Blackpool Operative House Painters," stating, that what the
book-keeper had done had come to their knowledge, and
desiring that he should not be allowed to do so again, "he
not being a painter."

Very many unions, in their anxiety to prevent over-
exertion, scarcely tolerate ordinary activity of movement.
They often show themselves scarcely less desirous that
masters should get as little as possible of their work done,
than that the men should get the highest possible pay for
the little they do. Making work is generally what they
really mean when they talk of doing work—a new distinction, unknown to the schoolmen, being thus pointed out
between *opus operans* and *opus operatum.* "Sometimes,"
says Mr G. F. Trollope, the eminent London builder, "I
have said to some of my men who were at work in the
joiners' shop. 'Now come, do you mean to call that a fair
day's work?' and the answer has been, 'Well, sir, it is
not, but I am not allowed to beat my mates.'" "I have
been quite surprised," says Mr George Smith, "knowing
what my own disposition would be, to see men working
down to so low a level, because it is more difficult to work
slowly, or to do anything else slowly, than to do it at proper
speed." Mr Trollope once asked a young man who was
walking along the street about two o'clock in the afternoon,
where he was going. "Oh, I am going to Mr So-and-so's
to work." And at what time do you expect to get there?
At the pace you are going, not, seemingly, till it will be
time to leave off." "I am very sorry, sir," was the man's
apology, "but we are not allowed to sweat ourselves if we
are walking in your time." "Not beating one's mates"
has by several unions been made the subject of special
enactment. "You are strictly cautioned," says a bye-law

of the Bradford Bricklayers' Labourers, "not to overstep good rules by doing double work, and causing others to do the same in order to gain a smile from the master. Such foolhardy and deceitful actions leave a great portion of good members out of employment. Certain individuals have been guilty, who will be expelled if they do not refrain." The Manchester Bricklayers' Association have a rule providing that 'any man found running or working beyond a regular speed shall be fined 2s. 6d. for the first offence, 5s. for the second, 10s. for the third, and if still persisting, shall be dealt with as the committee think proper." As also shall be "any man working short-handed, without man for man." In the building trade, working too fast is technically called "chasing." The Secretary of the Operative Masons being questioned as to its prohibition by his society, represented the object to be to prevent a man's destroying himself by over-exertion. He admitted, however, that a man of strength and skill so much above the average as to be able to do more and better work than his fellows without the slightest extra exertion on his part, would still be required to observe the same pace as they. He would have equally to conform to the injunction, "not to take up less time than an average mason in the execution of each description of work." Some anti-chasing regulations are, like this one, rather vaguely expressed. Others are explicit in defining what is to be understood by a proper or average quantity of work. At Liverpool, a bricklayer's labourer may legally carry as many as twelve bricks at a time. Elsewhere, ten is the greatest number allowed. But at Leeds " any brother in the union professing to carry more than the common number, which is eight bricks, shall be fined 1s. ; " and any brother " knowing the same without giving the earliest information thereof to the committee of management, shall be fined the same." At Birmingham, by agreement between masters and men, the number of bricks that may be carried varies with the height to which they are carried—so many to a first floor, so many less to a second floor, and so on, and generally different ladders are used for different floors. But one day an Irish labourer was caught by his master carrying only eight bricks to the first floor, yet insisted that he was in order. " Why," cries the master, "it is only the first floor." " Ah, shure," retorts Pat, " but then 'tis a three-storey ladder." At certain · places the labourers have ordained that bricks shall be carried only in hods, however preferable it might be to wheel them in barrows. At Birmingham, a master, who was doing some heavy work at the canal side, laid planks across from the boat, and wanted his labourers to wheel the bricks from the boat straight to the place where they were to be used; but the labourers would have none of such new-fangled notions, and threatened to strike if the bricks were not all unloaded in the ordinary way, and stacked on the canal side, and then carried by hod down to the works. Every reader may not have quite perceived what was meant when, a few sentences back, men were spoken of as not being allowed to sweat themselves if walking in their master's time. In most country districts, though not in London or its neighbourhood, it is an understood thing that when a man has to walk any distance to his work, half of the walking is to be treated as part of his day's labour, and paid for accordingly, the man usually walking one way in his own time, and the other in the master's time. Where the men are in the ascendant, however, they often put their own interpretation upon this understanding; sometimes they insist that every one employed at a distance from his master's headquarters shall be allowed walking time, even though he himself be living close by ; sometimes that all the men employed on the distant job shall meet at some common starting-point in order to walk from thence to their work, even though, in order to reach the place of rendezvous, they must pass their final destination.

It is when masters are entangled with time contracts which they are bound under heavy penalties to fulfil, yet cannot fulfil without the co-operation of their men, that they are most completely at the mercy of the latter, who too often use the opportunities so afforded them without shame or remorse. But, indeed, the strain which some unions habitually put upon the latter of their most extravagant regulations is, if possible, more preposterous than the regulations themselves. Neither do they shrink, when it suits them, from improvising a regulation for the nonce. According to the rules of the Glasgow Bricklayers' Association, 7d. an hour being the ordinary wage, overtime is to be paid as time and a-half, and Sabbath work as double time, and, in the case of a country job, the fare going and returning, and likewise full wages for the time spent in travelling, are to be paid by the employer. Under these rules, a bricklayer sent from Glasgow to Bristol claimed, for not quite nine days·spent upon the voyage there and back, £9, 13s. 7½d., exclusive of steamboat fare. The total was reached by charging full wages for all the ordinary working hours spent on board, charging all the nights as overtime, and two Sundays as partly double time and partly overtime, and charging in addition 1s. a day for twenty-eight and a quarter days, on account of having been for nine days, more than three miles distant from Glasgow Cross, and another shilling for each of the nights of the said nine days. The employer, astounded at the exorbitance of the claim, appealed against it to the union, and had the satisfaction of being laconically assured by the secretary in reply that " the charge was quite reasonable, and would require to be paid." Messrs Monteith, calico printers, of

Glasgow, engaged with a Mr Beeton for the plastering of a
house they were erecting. Beeton failed in the middle of
his contract, leaving one week's pay due to his workmen,
who continued to hang about the premises for another week,
without, however, doing any work. Messrs Monteith then
got authority from the Sheriff for Caird, another plasterer,
to finish the plastering; but the Plasterers' Union would
not let Mr Caird's men begin until Mr Beeton's men were
paid by the Monteiths, not only for the week for which
Beeton owed them, but also for the week in which they
had idled. And this case, monstrous as it may seem, is by
no means unique. It is quite common for unionists, after a
successful strike, to make it a condition of their resuming
work that they shall be paid full wages for the time they
have been on strike. During the building of the Manchester Law Courts, the bricklayers' labourers struck because they were desired to wheel bricks instead of carrying
them on their shoulders. In consequence of the labourers'
strike, time was lost by the bricklayers, who afterwards
claimed for the time so lost, and struck because refused. On
this occasion the joiners, without pretending to have any
grievance of their own, struck to support the bricklayers, on
condition of being subsidised out of the latter's funds."

APPENDIX C.

THERE is no sadder spectacle to be seen on earth than
the degeneracy of a great nation. And this sadness is
the greater when the degeneracy is not mere political
decay and descent from a position of supremacy and power,
but involves all the higher elements of a nation's life ;
when mind, morals, manners, and physical condition have
alike shared in the downward progress ; when the deterioration is scarcely more visible in the citizen than in the
man. But the sadness reaches its culminating point when
this degeneracy is observable in a new state and among a
young people ; when they display a marvellous vigour of constitution even in the very speed of the consuming malady ;
when their corruption is the result, not of the feebleness
and decrepitude of age, but of energies directed to no
noble aim, consecrated by no lofty purpose, and controlled
by no dominating and venerated law. And the spectacle
grows strange as well as sad when it appears that all this
grievous and disheartening retrogression has taken place in
spite of—perhaps partly in consequence of—a combination of advantages and facilities such as never before were
accumulated round the favoured path of any nation ;—all
the powers of a high civilisation brought to bear upon all
the resources of primeval nature ; all the learning, science,

M

and experience of the world's maturity placed unreservedly
at the disposal of the world's earliest and freshest youth;
boundless territory; boundless freedom; perfect security
from all control or interruption from without; an inheritance of vast intellectual wealth and of no intellectual
fetters; a genial spirit of chivalry in the South, blending
with and tempering an earnest and somewhat stern spirit
of religion in the North;—and the whole in possession of
a people sprung from the choicest race that in modern
times has dwelt upon the earth.

This perplexing and melancholy phenomenon has been
presented to us by the United States of North America
at the close of Mr Buchanan's administration, and no
Englishman who is not meanly malignant can dwell upon
the picture without grief and shame. It offers few temp-
tations to the journalist; and the sketch which we propose
to give would be too painful for us to have undertaken, but
for two considerations. First, the history of the rapid
deterioration of American character and institutions is full
of warning and instruction, especially to Englishmen; for
we share many of their faults and are exposed to many
of their dangers; what they were we were, and what they
are we may become, unless we study their career and
avoid their mistakes: it is impossible for our statesmen and
political philosophers to delve in any richer mine. And,
secondly, we are inclined to believe that the great Republic of the West has reached and passed its lowest
point; that henceforth its citizens and its public men will
turn over a new leaf and retrace their false steps; that
—by what means, at what rate, and through what vicis-
situdes of prosperity and tribulation, we cannot tell—
they will finally attain a social and political condition
of which they may be justly proud; that the date of
1861 will be their new Era and their Year of Grace;

—for we do not believe in the permanent decay and degradation of any modern nation, least of all a nation of the Anglo-Saxon race. For seventy years they have had their own way ; they have rejoiced, perhaps insolently, in their youth and strength ; they have walked in the way of their heart and in the sight of their eyes ; and they now find that God has brought them into judgment for their wilfulness, as he said he would. Now, just when they are able to see all the steps which have brought them to their present pass, a golden opportunity, arising out of their very errors, is afforded them of recovery and redemption ; and it cannot be but that so sagacious and resolute a people will seize it and turn it to account.

In the year 1790 Washington, the first President of the United States, had just been unanimously elected to guide and work the new federal constitution. That constitution had been carefully framed by a convention comprising all the wisest and purest patriots of the country, and had, in the judgment of every one, been rendered necessary by the confusion and almost anarchy into which the liberated provinces had fallen, for the want of some strong government and some adequate bond of union, very shortly after the acknowledgment of their independence in 1783. At this period the confederated states were *thirteen* in number ; their aggregate population was, as nearly as possible, *four millions ;* and of this amount 700,000 were African slaves. All the states held slaves, with the single exception of Massachusetts ; but all regarded slavery as an institution full of danger and discredit, sincerely to be deprecated and quietly to be got rid of, as soon as circumstances should permit. The constitution was, to all appearance, as sagacious a one as could have been devised. Its framers fore-

saw most of the political dangers to which the state would
be exposed, and guarded against them with great anxiety,
and apparently with great skill. They endeavoured to
secure the supremacy of law and purity in the administration of justice by the extraordinary and paramount powers
conferred on the Supreme Court, and by ordaining the
irremovability of the judges both in that and in all inferior
tribunals. They hoped to provide against the consequence
of too sudden and simultaneous a change in the governing
body by appointing the election of the chief of the executive
and the members of the legislative assemblies for different
terms and at different epochs. They provided a legitimate
time and means for the introduction of such changes as
experience might show to be desirable in the constitution
or as altered circumstances might necessitate, by enacting
the assembling of a Convention for the purpose of revision,
at certain distant intervals and under certain specified for-
malities. They fancied they had secured the choice of the
President by the wisest heads of the nation and in the most
dispassionate manner, by arranging a system of double
election, in virtue of which the nation's decision as to its
ruling head was vested in a small body of men chosen *ad
hoc* by the whole mass of the enfranchised people. They
endeavoured to give as much strength to the Federal executive as the jealous susceptibilities of democratic temper
in the several states would permit,—well aware that herein
lay the real weakness and the chief danger of the new
organisation,—by making the President supreme over all
appointments, and able to select and to retain his ministers
in defiance of hostile majorities in Congress. Finally, they
attempted to supply such barriers as seemed feasible under
republican institutions against the excessive preponderance
of the democratic element, by the adoption of those electoral qualifications which existed at the time in the several

states, which in some of them were stringent enough, and in all were a very decided and effectual negation of universal suffrage. A property qualification, or the payment of direct taxes, and usually a certain length of residence, was necessary to constitute a man an elector either for the Presidential Colleges, or for the Congress, or for the State Legislature. *In every state, with three exceptions,* as we shall hereafter see, *these sagacious provisions and securities have been swept away,* so that of the constitution framed by Washington, Franklin, Adams, Jefferson, Hamilton, and Randolph, little remains except the shell.

In Washington's hands the new political organisation worked well, and the Executive seemed almost strong enough. Such difficulties as arose even at that early stage of the experiment were easily surmounted by his promptitude, resolution, and prestige. But Washington was a man in a million. He achieved success in the two most arduous enterprises which can try the faculties of statesmen : he conducted a revolutionary war to a triumphant issue, with the smallest conceivable means and against the most powerful nation in the world ; and he inaugurated and administered for eight years a constitution peculiar, unprecedented, and in some points unavoidably and incurably defective from its origin. His embarrassments and the scantiness of his resources as a revolutionary chief have seldom been done justice to. Wellington's difficulties in the early days of his Peninsular campaigns, though analogous in some respects and formidable enough, were trivial in comparison. The American Revolution presented many features which distinguished it from most other movements of a similar nature, and added enormously to the obstacles and complications with which its leaders had to contend. In the first place, during all its earlier stages, it was not a revolution at all, or even a rebellion. It was merely a resistance in the name of law and constitutional right to an illegal exercise of power. For many years the colonists had no idea of assailing, much less of overthrowing, the king's authority : they merely aimed at confining it within legitimate bounds. There was in consequence every degree of difference of opinion as to the extent to which resistance should be pushed, and the means by which it was to be carried on. The great majority of the colonists were sincerely attached to the mother country, were even ardent in their loyalty, and were shocked at the bare notion of rebellion or separation ; and these sentiments continued to animate them up to a very late period of the contest. Thus the chiefs of the movement had to guide and to act for a people who were any thing but united in their sentiments and purposes, and whose views moreover were in a constant state of fluctuation and of progressive development.

Then, again, when resistance had become general and resolute, when all word of compromise or submission was over, and when ulterior plans and hopes began to present themselves to a few of the more advanced and excited spirits, the very simplicity and purity of the motives which led to the rebellion placed serious barriers in the way of its success. It was resistance in the name of a sacred principle, not revolt against cruel and unendurable oppression. It was carried on to assert a constitutional right, not to escape from or resent a hideous wrong. The tax to which the colonists refused to submit was a mere trifle : no one would have felt its pressure ; no one would have refused or grudged its payment, had it but been legitimately levied. The colonists had no atrocious tyranny to escape from ; justice was purely administered ; their property was secure ; their personal liberty was never menaced ; their religion and their claims of conscience never came in question. They had every thing they could wish for, as far as practical freedom and the daily enjoyments of life were concerned ; but they would not be taxed without their own consent, even to the extent of a few shillings per head ; and for this they went to war. Now, it is evident that a motive of this sort, honourable and defensible as it may be, is very inferior in stimulating and sustaining power to those barbarous and unjust tyrannies, and that burning passion for emancipation and revenge, which have usually caused nations to rise in armed rebellion against their rulers. It may suffice to make men vote, harangue, combine, go to prison for a while perhaps ; seldom to make them—seldomer still to make them cheerfully—endure severe privations, or encounter with unflinching spirit the sacrifices and hardships inseparable from a prolonged and dubious strife. The origin of the rebellion thus goes far to explain the general backwardness and lukewarmness of which Washington had so frequently occasion to complain. Had the colonists suffered more, and had more reason for resistance, their emancipation would have been incomparably easier.

But, besides all this, Washington, properly speaking, had no army, no authority, no means, no government. He had literally to make bricks without straw. The colonies hitherto had been entirely distinct and unconnected with each other ; they were unaccustomed to combined action ; and the assembly of delegates improvised for the occasion was without constituted authority, and therefore without power. They could appoint Washington their commander-in-chief but that was about all. They could not compel his officers to obey him ; they could not compel soldiers to flock to his standard ; they could not compel citizens to administer to the necessities of his army. They could authorise him to make requisitions, but they could not

empower him to enforce them, nor oblige the several states
to recognise them.   They could not legally contract loans
nor levy taxes.   They could only decide what contributions
should be called for, and *recommend* and urge the people of
each state to give their quota cheerfully.   Persuasion, both
at the seat of government and at the head-quarters of the
army, had to do the work of authority.   Washington himself, as well as the civil leaders, had to raise the sinews of
war by argument, by entreaty, by remonstrance, by personal influence, in short.   Merchants, planters, magistrates,
officers, sent in loans and contributions as they could or as
they felt moved to do.   The contest was, in fact, very
much carried on *by subscription;* and this had to be done
for years.   In the army itself nearly the same state of
affairs prevailed.   The soldiers were in a manner volunteers.   They enlisted only for a time ; desertion seemed
almost legal, since it was only desertion from a rebel force ;
they felt themselves in a manner at liberty to disband when
they were weary, or had fought through one campaign, or
when domestic or agricultural concerns wanted their
presence at home ; and thus they sometimes dispersed just
when a victory had to be turned to account, or a defeat to
be repaired, or a promising enterprise to be undertaken.
Then the soldiers often chose their own officers, and would
obey no others.   All orders and plans were freely discussed ;
the commander-in-chief had to *persuade* his regimental
colonels rather than to direct them ; his army was more
of a voluntary association than an organised body of troops.
Power there was almost none ; authority could do little ;
personal influence, moral and intellectual qualities, had to
do the work of both.   And all this time,—while Washington had to control his men, to exhort his officers, to beg
sometimes almost piteously for supplies,—he had to fight
more numerous and powerful antagonists, whom nothing

but the imbecility of their commanders could have enabled him to overcome; and to contend against the mean jealousies, the ill-timed parsimony, and the ungenerous exigencies and suspicions of his fellow-citizens. Nay, more, he had to keep together, and to inspire with zeal and submission to needful discipline, an army often without food, usually without pay, always unsupported by magazines and stores, yet sternly forbidden to supply their wants by plunder or exactions. Truly here was a field, such as few men have, for the exercise of that hopeful and untiring patience which is perhaps the sublimest and most difficult of virtues ; and never w..; there a more magnificent example of this attribute than Washington. His military genius was no doubt great ; but it was as nothing compared with the moral qualities which were required to bear up against those difficulties which deprived military genius of its fairest opportunities. His reputation was founded, not on splendid days, but on painful years ; not on a series of those brilliant and startling achievements in which, if there is much of inspiration, there is often yet more of accident ; but on a whole life of toil, sacrifice, self-control, and self-abnegation, such as no man can lead whose principles and whose virtues are not rooted in the very deepest recesses of his nature.

His sagacity in governing the State was as eminent as his ability in·creating it. For eight years he ruled the young commonwealth with rare prudence and firmness, showing the same resolute front to domestic insubordination as to foreign encroachment ; and when he retired in 1796 to the private happiness he had so long sighed for, he left behind him that farewell address which is perhaps the most touching legacy of wisdom and affection ever bequeathed by a ruler to his native land. The exhortation shows with how true a foresight he laid his finger on each one of the dangers and weaknesses of the Republic. He

warns his countrymen against "geographical divisions,"—
against the bad habit, even as a phrase, of speaking of *the
North* and *the South*. He tells them that to be a NATION,
they must have a central government, which should be the
chief object of their loyalty, and which no local or democratic jealousies should be allowed to weaken ; but he does
this in language which proves how doubtful he felt in his
heart whether the Union could permanently be preserved.
" Let experience solve the question," he says ; " to listen
to mere speculation in such a case were criminal." He
exhorts them earnestly to uphold public credit and the
strictest national integrity at any cost, by careful economy
and cheerful acquiescence in necessary taxes. Finally, he
recommends a policy of rigid neutrality towards foreign
countries, peace, forbearance, but above all the most mag-
nanimous and scrupulous justice and good faith ; and,
knowing his countrymen, he assures them that in the long-
run this policy, and this alone, will *pay*.

By the universal consent of mankind, Washington stands
out among statesmen as the wisest, best, and purest ruler
who ever governed a free nation. He was pre-eminent, no
doubt, among his colleagues and countrymen both in wisdom
and in virtue, but he had many wise and virtuous men to
assist him in his work. Jefferson, Hamilton, Randolph,
Jay, Madison, and Adams, though holding very different
opinions, were all earnest and high-minded patriots. The
first among them did ultimately much harm by the uncom-
promising democracy of his principles ; but they were all
worthy coadjutors of their noble chief. There were giants
in those days ; there are only dwarfs now. What are the
advantages, and what should be the future of a nation
which started on its career with such a man as Washington
for its representative and guide !

Pass over forty years from the opening of the first presidency of Washington, and we come to 1830, when Andrew Jackson was the Chief of the United States. At this date the area of the country had been augmented from 820,000 square miles to 1,786,000, by the cession of Louisiana and the seizure of Florida. The number of Confederated States had multiplied from *thirteen* to *twenty-four;* the total population had swelled from *four* millions to *thirteen* millions, and the slaves from 700,000 to 2,000,000. The Free States now constituted twelve out of the twenty-four States. The total commerce of the country—the annual imports and exports—had increased from 72,000,000$ in 1790 to 144,000,000$ in 1830.

The change is enormous : territory, commerce, and number of commonwealths doubled; population trebled. But the moral, social, and political change during these forty years was even more startling still, and unfortunately was not in an equally encouraging direction. In the first place, the formal and recognised modifications in the institutions of the country between the time of Washington and the time of Jackson were neither few nor trifling ; and all tended to increase the uncontrolled power of the popular will, and were so many progressive encroachments of democracy. In 1790 every State required certain property qualifications from their citizens before endowing them with the electoral franchise: they were obliged either to be freeholders or leaseholders to a specified amount, or to pay a fixed sum in direct taxes, or to possess personal property of some sort. These wise precautions did not last long. Not a single State whose constitution was framed since 1800 requires any property qualification for the exercise of the suffrage ; and in most of the older States the established qualifications were greatly reduced, and universal, or quasi-universal, suffrage was adopted,—by Massachusetts in

1821; by Connecticut in 1818; by New York in 1821 and 1826; by Maryland in 1801 and 1809; by Virginia in 1830; by Mississippi in 1833; and by Tennessee in 1835. Now, when we remember that the electors for the State Legislatures are also electors for the House of Representatives in Congress, and that the Federal Senate is chosen by the State Legislatures, we shall become aware how effectually this democratic progress must have made itself felt not only in the Provincial, but in the National Assemblies.

In the course of the same period the first steps were taken towards a still more fatal innovation in the Judiciary system. That the independence of judges is essential to the pure administration of justice and to the security of true freedom, and that this independence must be jealously guarded, and can only be effectually secured by appointing the judges for life or during good behaviour, have always been regarded as unassailable maxims of sound policy. They were adopted and followed, as we have seen, by the framers of the Federal Constitution. But scarcely twelve years had elapsed, ere a notion had grown up in the minds of some ultra-democrats, among whom we are grieved to have to name Jefferson, that irremovable and independent authorities of any kind were fetters and incongruities in a truly popular government; and preparations were made, with only too easy success, for bringing courts of justice, like every other institution, under the direct control of the people. In 1802, under Jefferson's auspices (our authority in these matters is Justice Story), sixteen duly-appointed judges were dismissed, and their courts abolished by an act of Congress, without notice and without compensation. The same President pertinaciously urged the limitation of judicial appointments to terms of four or six years, *renewable by the President and Senate,*—thus reducing their holders to a state of absolute dependence. Jackson adopted the same fatal notion, and recommended it to Congress in 1829 and in 1832 ; and before his tenure of office ceased *five* out of the twenty-four states then existing had gone even a step farther, and *made the judges elective*, and elective only for a term of years.

Another unimportant but significant movement had been made during the same period. The payment of representatives has always, for obvious reasons, been regarded as a specially democratic scheme. It had been naturally enough incorporated with the Federal constitution of 1789, by which members of Congress were paid *six* dollars a day during actual attendance on their duties, besides an equal allowance, under the name of " mileage," for every twenty miles of distance from their residence. In 1795 the payment was raised (though shortly afterwards again reduced) to *seven* dollars. In 1816, instead of six dollars a day, they voted themselves 1500 dollars a year. But this would appear to have been unpopular with their constituents, for the vote was repealed the following year ; and in 1821 the payment was finally fixed at *eight* dollars a day during session, with eight dollars for " mileage."

Again, the democratic instinct—than which nothing is keener or surer—had contrived effectually to neutralise, without formally repealing, that provision of the constitution which endeavoured to place the election of the President in the hands of " select men," by enacting that he should be chosen by a body of men elected *ad hoc*. The reason of this provision, according to Judge Story, was, that such a body " would be most likely to possess the information, discernment, and independence essential for the proper discharge of this duty,"—and, according to Justice Kent, " to close the opportunity as much as possible against negotiation, intrigue, and corruption." How entirely this purpose has been frustrated we shall see presently ; but, even in the period we are now speaking of, it was virtually evaded. " It is notorious," says Mr Story, " that these [presidential] electors are now chosen wholly with reference to particular candidates, and are silently pledged to vote for them. Nay, upon some occasions the electors publicly pledge themselves to vote for a particular person ; and thus, in effect, the whole foundation of the system so elaborately constructed is subverted ; . . . . and nothing is left to the electors after their nomination but to register votes which are already pledged ; and *an exercise of an independent judgment would be treated as a political usurpation,* dishonourable to the individual and a fraud upon his constituents."

Finally, it was reserved for General Jackson to give the most desperate and fatal blow to the dignity and purity of republican government in America ever inflicted upon it by friend or foe. By one single act he may almost be said to have effected the ruin of his country. Up to his time all the government *employés,* civil and military, with a very 'few specified exceptions, held office in the United States, as in England, during life and good behaviour, were never removed for their political opinions, and never changed with any change of administration. The justice as well as the policy of this practice is too obvious to be dwelt upon. By the constitution the control over all these offices, as well as the appointment to them, was vested in the chief of the Executive, the sanction of the Senate being required in only a few cases ; but it is worthy of remark that this absolute power over the government *employés* was only conferred upon the President after long discussion and by a very narrow majority. The clause affirming it only passed the Senate by the casting-vote of the vice-president ; and in the long debates that it gave rise to, the idea that any chief of the State could so far disgrace himself and damage the community as to abuse the power conferred for personal or electioneering purposes, was scouted as an insult and a chimera. Nor was it abused till the advent of the violent and unprincipled ruler whose era we are now considering. During Washington's eight years of administration, he only removed *nine* persons from office,—one, a foreign minister, at the instance of the French Directory ; the other eight for cause assigned. Politics had nothing to do with any of the cases. Adams also removed *nine* subordinate officers, but none for political reasons. Jefferson removed *thirty-nine*, but, as he solemnly declared and was ready to prove, not one of them because their political opinions differed from his own. Indeed, his purity in the matter of appointments almost approached to prudery. Madison made *five* removals ; Monroe, *nine ;* John Quincey Adams, *two* only. General Jackson was no sooner inaugurated than *he dismissed from office nearly every man who had opposed him or whose friends had voted for his opponent, and replaced them by partisans of his own.* The number thus removed was variously stated : his enemies mentioned *two thousand ;* his friends admitted *six hundred and ninety.* We are content to accept the moderate and indisputable account of Justice Story, who specifies 8 in the diplomatic corps ; 36 in the executive department ; 190 in other civil departments ; besides 491 postmasters. " These officers," he says, " included a very large proportion of all the most lucrative offices under the national government."

It is impossible to exaggerate, and needless to point out in detail, the ruinous results which must flow from such a course of proceeding,—a course which, once inaugurated, must almost necessarily be continued, since its adoption by one party or one President compels its imitation by the antagonistic faction as a measure at once of justice and of self-defence. Accordingly, this plan of wholesale removals

has been pursued ever since, and is now the common practice. At each presidential election the whole places in the
gift of the government, from the highest to the lowest,
change hands. The consequences are manifold, and all
mischievous. *First*, few men can obtain any skill or experience in their office, and the official capacity of the civil
service must be deplorably impaired. *Secondly*, every man,
knowing that he has only a four years' (or at most, and by
every exertion, an eight years') tenure of place, will be
inclined to " feather his nest " as fast and as daringly as he
can. *Thirdly*, public appointments are thus converted into
an engine of jobbery and corruption on the grandest scale
and of the dirtiest sort. Every office is promised, and is
promised in return for political support. There is nowhere
in the world bribery and electioneering intrigue comparable
for openness and shamelessness to that of the United States.
And *fourthly* (and worst perhaps of all), it renders it impossible for men of intelligence, ability, and virtue, who wish
for a reasonable permanence and a decent independence, to
become servants of the State. Office necessarily falls into
the hands of a very third-rate class of men. One American
writer sums the matter up by the assertion, that, " in the
year of our Lord 1859, the fact of a man's holding (remov-
able) office under the government is presumptive evidence
that he is one of three characters, viz., an adventurer, an
incompetent person, or a scoundrel."

Such were the inroads made upon the wise policy of the
previous generation as far as the constitution was concerned.
A similar departure from Washington's principle of action
in external questions had already manifested itself. Those
projects of conquest and annexation which have now made
such fearful progress had already entered deeply into the
national mind, and received the tacit, if not formal, sanction

of the executive. General Jackson had already conquered Florida from the Spaniards, as the issue of a war of which, to say the least, the success was more indisputable than the justice ; and this conquest did as much towards rendering him the favourite of the people as his military triumphs over the Indian tribes or his defence of New Orleans against the British. In Colonel Burr's filibustering scheme against Texas in 1806, he is said to have heartily sympathised. He attempted to obtain this province by negotiation in 1829, and was unquestionably at least *cognisant* of Houston's plans for effecting that gradual seizure of Texas from Mexico, which was designed to end, first, in her independence, and then in her annexation to the United States. He certainly offered no impediments to the execution of Houston's scheme: the last year of his presidency saw the first part of the drama fully played out; and before he died he deliberately counselled the consummation of the unprincipled and long-planned piracy. This was the first practical inauguration of those doctrines of "manifest destiny," which have ever since been at once the opprobrium and the chief prospective danger of the American Republic.

Another point of difference between the era of Washington and the era of Jackson is, that the question of Slavery— which was scarcely noticed in 1790, and which, in its direct or inferential issues, was the overshadowing and all-absorbing interest in 1860—had already made its difficulties felt in the arena of American politics. The decision as to the extension of those limits within which slavery was to be permitted had already been fiercely contested on the occasion of the admission of Missouri into the Union in 1820, and settled by a compromise, which was to have been unalterable, but which we have recently seen most questionably set aside. In Jackson's own presidency we hear little of the subject, for it was never brought directly into

N

issue on any question of practical policy ; but it painfully occupied the minds of all thoughtful statesmen ; and it had become obvious that, apart from all considerations as to the continuance of such a social blot upon the national character, it was ripening fast into a desperate controversy as to the balance of power, or rather the possession of supremacy, between the North and the South. The ambition of the South and the conscience and fears of the North were growing more and more restless during the whole of this apparent truce ; and the existence of two millions of a servile race disturbed and perplexed minds which had looked with easy indifference on a coloured population of 700,000, destined, as it was thought, to early and gradual emancipation.

In Jackson's time, too, we trace the rise of what has since been one of the most disgraceful features of the social and public life of the United States,—a feature significant of terrible and growing barbarism. We refer to those brutal assaults of eminent citizens and public men on one another, in open places and even in official sanctuaries, which have been the opprobrium of nearly all the newer and southern states, and which culminated in the cowardly attack by Mr Brooks on Mr Sumner in the senate-house at Washington. These assaults in themselves might pass as the mere ebullitions of brutal passions : their *impunity*, which began in Jackson's time, tells a more serious tale. In 1832, the well-known General Houston, afterwards the filibuster and governor of Texas, found fault with some sharp criticisms made upon a transaction in which he was involved. The words were spoken by Mr Stanberry of Ohio, in the House of Representatives at Washington, of which he, as well as Houston, was a member. Houston met his critic in the street, assailed him with a bludgeon in one hand and a pistol in the other, struck him from behind, felled him to the ground, and then *continued beating him* long after he was able to offer any resistance, and till a bystander—Senator Buckner of Missouri, who watched *the whole process without attempting to interfere or seeming ashamed of his quiescence*—thought he was killed. The outrage was reported to the Speaker, was investigated *in spite of the efforts of James Polk (afterwards President) to smother inquiry*, and ended in Houston being reprimanded in so mild a manner as to leave little doubt that the Speaker sympathised with the assailant rather than with the victim.

This was bad enough ; but it was not the worst. Jackson, then President, defended his blackguard friend, saying, that "after a few more examples of the same kind, members of Congress would perhaps learn to keep civil tongues in their heads." He did more : when the district court of Columbia sentenced Houston to pay $500 for the offence, Jackson actually *nullified the sentence and remitted the fine !* Such was the man who, in 1832, sat in the seat of Washington. Of course such an example, with such encouragement, bore speedy fruit. Another member of Congress, Mr Arnold, who had commented severely on Houston's brutality, was twice publicly assaulted by a Major Heard, a friend of Houston's, who struck him with a club and fired a pistol at him, as usual taking him unawares, and as usual, also, committing the outrage in the presence of sympathising or indifferent spectators.

This circumstance alone would suffice to depict the character of the man who was twice chosen to be the chief of the great Republic, and who was certainly the most popular President since Washington. He was simply a violent, ignorant, narrow-minded man, of boundless self-confidence and iron will ; bitter in his enmities, rooted in his prejudices, intemperate alike in conduct and in language. He was unrelenting towards every one who ever opposed him, and unscrupulous in his mode of effecting his revenge. He treated the Congress no better than the Bank. He dismissed any of his ministers who differed from him just as cavalierly as he had dismissed the office-holders whose friends had voted against him. He removed the government deposits from the United States Bank, and did his best to destroy that institution, because he fancied its influence had been employed to prevent his election. Long before he became President he had put two Englishmen to death in Florida, on a most scantily sustained charge of exciting the Indians against his troops ; and when the court-martial to which he had consigned them sentenced one of them only to a flogging, Jackson, on his own authority, ordered the unhappy victim to be shot. His one merit appears to have been his unflinching resolution. He was a democratic despot ; and unhappily the American people had already, as they progressed in democracy, begun to have a taste for despotism. The leading politicians of his day, Clay, Calhoun, and Webster, were men of great ability and power—Webster especially, who lacked nothing but character and purity of patriotism ; they were vastly superior to their master—vastly superior, too, in all respects to those who have been leaders since ; but at an immeasurable distance below Washington, Hamilton, Jefferson, and Jay.

Pass now over thirty years more, to the presidency of Mr Buchanan in 1860. By the annexation of Texas, by the Treaty of Oregon, and by seizures (afterwards confirmed by treaty) from Mexico, the total area of the states had expanded from 1,786,000 to 2,963,000 square miles. The two territories, Texas and New Mexico, acquired by fraud or violence from their southern neighbours, exceeded in extent the whole area of the United States at the date of their separation from England. The number of confederated commonwealths in the Union had multiplied from *twenty-four* to *thirty-three*, of which eighteen were free ; the total population was 31,600,000 in place of 13,000,000 ; and just four millions out of the thirty-one were slaves. Meanwhile the aggregate foreign commerce of the country, which was $72,000,000 in 1700, and $144,000,000 in 1830, had reached the enormous figure of $700,000,000 in 1859.

But vast as are these changes in the lapse of one generation, others ·have taken place in the same period quite as startling, and by no means as satisfactory. We are giving a sketch only—not a history ; we will, therefore, be as brief and graphic as we can, overlaying our picture with but few details, and referring our readers for proofs and statistics to more elaborate publications. In the first place, then, we have to notice that the gradual reduction or abolition of all qualifications for the exercise of electoral rights in the several states, which had already proceeded so far in 1830, has now been almost everywhere consummated. In only about ten states is even the semblance of any restriction on universal suffrage yet maintained, and in most of these it is but a semblance. In twenty-one of the most populous and powerful states, every free male white of the age of twenty years, who shall have resided for some short period varying from three months to two years, is entitled to vote, though he neither serves the militia, nor pays a single tax, nor possesses a dollar of property real or personal. Contemporaneous with this change, and naturally connected with it, is the increase and now universal prevalence of a most mischievous practice, viz., that elections have fallen into the hands of professional agents, who devote themselves to the business, and work the whole machinery for the candidates who employ them ; who spare neither calumny, intimidation, promises, nor bribes ; and who are, as might be anticipated, among the most noxious class of bankrupt and disreputable rowdies. This is no loose or unwarranted statement ; all thoughtful patriots in the Union have long deplored the evil ; the American press teems with instances ; and governors of states (New York especially) have repeatedly called attention to the fact, but have proved wholly powerless to repress it.*

In Jackson's time, as we have seen, the first blow had been struck at the purity and independence of the judicial bench. In 1833, *five* states out of twenty-four had taken the fatal step of appointing their judges by popular election, and for only a limited term of office. This grievous error, so irresistibly tempting to the capricious and despotic temper of democracies, made terribly rapid progress. In 1844, the five had swelled to *twelve ;* and now (we quote from Mr Tremenheere) " the elective principle in the appointment of judges, and their appointment for short periods, prevails in *twenty-two* states in the Union. In *three* others the elective principle has been adopted, but the term is during good behaviour ; and in two others they are appointed for a term of years by the governor." In New York the dependence of the judges of the superior courts is secured by rendering their salaries subject to an annual vote of the Legislature. The consequences of these ultra-democratic provisions are obvious enough. In the first

---

* See Mr Tremenheere's two volumes, especially i. 129, and ii. 123. One of the most striking proofs of the progress of democratic encroachment, and of submission to it, may be found in the fact that at the recent presidential election one, at least, of the candidates, and that one the most eminent (Mr Douglas), *for the first time* in the history of the United States, stooped to what is called " stumping ; " *i.e.*, making canvassing speeches to the mob, wherever a crowd collected on his progress. He spoke sometimes at railway stations, sometimes from the balconies of hotels, sometimes from improvised platforms. This fact we heard from a gentleman who occasionally travelled with him, and knew him well.

place, no first-rate lawyers will aspire to or accept a position at once so precarious and so undignified ; and the bench will be, and often is, filled by men inferior in all qualities to the members of the bar over whom they preside, but from whom, of course, they cannot command respect. In the next place, it is inevitable that judicial decisions will tend to bear the impress of the popular passions and desires, instead of acting as a salutary check upon them. Judges who canvass for their seats can scarcely be severe or strictly impartial with those who elect them ; the plaintiff in the case or the prisoner at the bar will be able to remind the presiding justice that he voted for him ; and the magistrate will find it difficult to pronounce judgment against popular violence and prejudice when he knows that such judgment will infallibly cost him his salary and his post. Nor is this a merely conjectural apprehension : the celebrated Van Renselaer, or Anti-Rent, struggle at Albany was a case in point ; decision after decision was given in favour of the plaintiff, whose legal rights were indisputable, but none of them could be enforced by the executive authorities ; till at last, after many trials and judical changes, a tribunal was found which gave judgment in accordance with the dictates of democratic greed. It was in reference to this case that the *successful* candidate for the office of Attorney-General of the State of New York, in his canvass, publicly and in writing, pledged himself to support the popular view by every legal means within his power. A somewhat similar case occurred some years ago in Massachusetts. The Ursuline Convent at Charlestown, near Boston, was attacked by the mob, without any provocation from the harmless nuns, pillaged, and destroyed by fire. Vigorous efforts were made to bring the offenders to justice, but in vain. In spite of the clearest evidence, jury after jury acquitted them, for no reason except that the Catholics, and especially the

Irish Catholics, were unpopular in Boston.* Several numbers since, the *National Review* cited the case of the Erie
Railway outrages described by Mr Chambers, wherein *the
mayor and his officers* were the rioters, and wantonly tore
up the rails of an unpopular company, whose only offence
was that they proposed to pass through the town without
making it a stopping-station. The spectators quietly sympathised with the lawless destroyers, and no justice could
be obtained, the violators of the law being themselves the
elected of the people. A more recent specimen of the same
temper occurred, as we all remember, at Staten Island, New
York, two years ago, when the Quarantine Hospital was
destroyed with perfect impunity, the patients having been
forcibly removed and *laid down outside*, by a mob composed
of the principal inhabitants, who chose to regard it as a
nuisance, and, being unable to remove it by process of law,
chose this summary and scandalous method of enforcing
their arbitrary will.

It is curious to observe how this lawlessness is sometimes
exercised in the interests of law, or at least of order and
good government. Indeed the one encouraging feature of
society in the United States is the latent *power of rectification*—the tendency of an evil, when it becomes flagrant and
intolerable, to work its own cure. For a long time, as is
well known, there has been a growing disposition to allow
all administrative affairs, small as well as great, to fall into
the worst hands,—into the hands, that is, of men who make
politics not a profession but a trade, a handicraft, a money-
making and lucrative occupation,—the idle, the violent, the
irregular, and the damaged. The cause of this is twofold:
first, the more respectable and industrious men are busy in
their own callings, and are too engrossed in the fierce race
and struggle of competition to think much about public

* Grattan's "Civilised America," i. 141.

matters except when compelled to do so by the endangering
of their private concerns ; and, secondly, the best men are
too proud, too honest, and too firm to be popular with a
wilful and tyrannous majority, and therefore seldom offer
themselves for election, and are still more seldom chosen.
But when, in consequence of these operating influences, the
administration has fallen into the hands of men *too* rowdy-
ish, *too* infamous, or *too* incapable to be endured for very
shame ; or when these officials push their atrocities or their
corruptions beyond the very liberal line which even American tolerance has drawn,—then the respectability of the
community arouses itself like a giant for temporary action,
convulsive but irresistible, and the abusers of power are
kicked out with ignominy. Such is the explanation of those
" Vigilance Committees" of which we heard so much a few
years ago. One instance of their operation in California
will be sufficient to characterise the class. That province,
as was natural after the gold discoveries, speedily attracted
both all the adventurous energy and all the adventurous
rascality of the States : the former went to the diggings ;
the latter took possession of the administration. But after
a while the conduct of the official rowdies became so scandalous, crime grew so rife and so daring, and so certain of
impunity from the connivance or participation of those
whom packed ballot-boxes had placed in power, that a
" Vigilance Committee" was formed as a measure of self-
defence by a democratic community against a democratic
government. A public man of the name of Casey had made
himself conspicuous by some official misdeeds ; and the respectable editor of a respectable newspaper, Mr King, in
denouncing these transactions, reminded the public that
Casey was a " convict," and had served his time in Pennsylvania Penitentiary. Casey went to King and shot him
dead on his own door-step. He was arrested and sent to

gaol ; but as Mr King was very much respected, and as it
was notorious that any malefactor left in the hands of the
authorities would be either acquitted or allowed to escape,
the Vigilance Committee collected their adherents, planted
a cannon against the prison-door, and demanded the surrender of Casey and another murderer. The gaoler was
obliged to give them up : they were forthwith tried by a
sort of drum-head court-martial, and as their guilt was
notorious, they were hanged without delay. A number of
other well-known scoundrels were then ordered to quit the
place within twenty-four hours on pain of death ; a few
vigorous examples were made ; order, if not law, again prevailed ; and the community slept in security once more.
The truth is, that everywhere in America, the populace is
above the law : when the law acts too slowly or in an unpopular direction, it is superseded in the most cavalier
fashion, sometimes for good and sometimes for ill ; but in
any case, the administration is autocratic, not legal—
actually, often—*potentially*, at any moment. These exertions of arbitrary force, though often outrageously iniquitous,
may sometimes be necessary and are sometimes unquestionably righteous; but, just or unjust, they are undeniably
features of barbarism, not of civilisation ; and as such,
must be included among the evidences of relapse and
retrogression since the days of Washington.

We have already adverted to the mode in which the
election of the President is now conducted, and the deviation in practice from the original plan marked out by the
constitution. But the subject is curious, and calls for one
remark further. With a view, no doubt, to secure as far
as might be, that the individual who is to wield for four
years the very enormous power vested in the chief magistrate of the United States should be truly the choice of the

great body of the people, and not merely of a considerable portion of them, which might still be only a minority of the whole, the framers of the constitution enacted that the successful candidate must have not merely *more* votes than any competitor, but an *absolute* majority of the entire number of suffrages ; and that if no candidate secured this absolute majority, the choice should devolve upon the House of Representatives. This provision has produced exactly the opposite effect from that designed. It has almost secured that the President chosen shall never be the one desired or designed by the popular voice. The *modus operandi* is well worth notice, and will explain—far better than the supposed ostracism of superiority to which it is usually attributed— the reason why the eminent politicians of the United States so rarely reach the presidential chair. It is obvious that if *several* candidates were allowed to appear in the field, the chances of any one of them obtaining an absolute majority would be small indeed, and that in consequence the choice would, as a rule, be taken from the people and handed over to the Congress. In order to provide against this unwelcome result, each of the two (or three) parties holds a convention, at which it is decided by repeated ballots which of the many aspirants shall be put forward as *the* candidate of the party, the ballots being continued till some one name receives an *absolute* majority of suffrages. Of course it usually happens that the two most eminent men,—the two favourites, have each of them so many votes, that neither has the required number ; and when it is made obvious by repeated trials that this negative result will continue, one of the favourites is withdrawn by his friends ; but as it would not be in human nature that they should vote for his antagonist, they usually give their suffrages to some comparitively obscure candidate, who thus finds himself unexpectedly possessed of the necessary number of votes. Even in the most recent case, Mr Lincoln, at the first two ballots, had fewer votes than Mr Seward. But the most remarkable and instructive illustration of the actual working of the provision we are considering occurred in 1852. The name of the candidate who was ultimately successful (Mr Pierce) did not even appear on the list till the thirty-fifth ballot. Sometimes Mr Cass had had the greatest number of votes, sometimes Mr Douglas, sometimes Mr Buchanan ; but Mr Pierce was an unknown man, of whom no one had ever dreamed. At the forty-eighth ballot he had only 55 votes out of 288 ; when, it appearing that the convention would never agree to the selection of any one of the favourite competitors, they tacitly agreed to meet as it were on neutral ground, and on the forty-ninth and last ballot Mr Pierce was nominated by 283 suffrages,—that is, almost unanimously. Nearly the same thing took place some years before, when Mr Polk, of whom no one had ever heard, was chosen in preference to the celebrated and really able Mr Clay, simply because he was an unknown man, who had no enemies and no rivals.

But perhaps the most remarkable change between the days of Andrew Jackson and those of Buchanan is the prominence assumed by the Slavery question, not so much in itself as in its indirect issues. For many years it has directed the whole policy of the Union and coloured the whole character of the people ; and it has done this much more from the political and economic, than from the moral, considerations immediately involved. It is very important that we should understand and bear in mind this distinction, if we would rightly comprehend the present strange crisis of American affairs. When we think and speak of the FREE STATES and the SLAVE STATES we are apt to fancy that the southerners are all slaveholders and the northerners are all abolitionists. This is as far from being the case as possible. Slavery is not looked upon there, as a rule, at all in the same light as with us. The citizens of New England, New York, and Pennsylvania, do not, as we do, regard the institution of slavery as an abomination and a sin, from which the nation should purge itself at any cost ; nor do they view the African race with that gushing and abounding pity which melts the heart of every Englishman. There is among them, no doubt, a considerable and perhaps an increasing body of " abolitionists," in our sense of the word, full of martyr courage, of martyr zeal, and often of martyr recklessness too, who will hold no parley with the unclean thing. But these men are comparatively few : they are not popular even at the North. As a rule, the free communities abhor the Negro, and sympathise little with his sufferings. But they see and have long felt that between communities worked .by free labour and communities worked by slave labour there is, and must be, an innate and extending diversity of interest : the two systems beget different characters and stimulate different desires. What can there be permanently in common between republican societies in which labour is held in honour, and republican societies in which it is held in disgrace—between those in which it is a passport to consideration and to power, and those in which it is a badge of servitude and degradation; The South feels this just as keenly as the North ; and the people there, believing themselves to be really superior to their northern brethren, have long watched with bitterness and envy—which has now grown into dismay and fury— the more rapid progress of the latter in wealth, in numbers, and in political preponderance. We need not go into the often-repeated comparison. In the days of Washington the free and the slave states were as nearly equal as possible in every assignable element of prosperity, except in climate, in

which the South had a marked advantage. *Now*, after the
lapse of seventy years, the slave states are only fifteen to
eighteen ; their white population is less than half, or
8,500,000 against 19,000,000 ; the number of representatives they send to Congress is scarcely more than half, being
84 against 150 ; the agricultural produce of the free states
is out of all proportion greater than that of the slave states;
their commerce is at least fourfold ; they contribute more
than five-sixths to the federal revenue derived from customs
duties ; nearly all the trade and industry of the South is
carried on by northern capital ; the postal administration
leaves a large surplus in the North and a large deficit in
the South ; the railroads in the two sections admit of no
comparison whatever ; and to complete the picture, the
comparative education in the free states is at least as
preponderant as their enterprise and their wealth.

This vast preponderance on the part of the free or northern
states, besides being, in itself, in a high degree mortifying
and irritating to the fiery spirits of the South, obviously
menaced their political equality—much more that supremacy which they had hitherto enjoyed, and had exercised
with such peremptory insolence. It was obvious that whenever the free states should think fit to act in conjunction
and with any near approach to unanimity, they would be
able to command the whole federal policy, and to appoint to
all places of trust, authority, or lucre, throughout the entire
Union. This was naturally a most unwelcome future; and
it was the more annoying and infuriating from two additional circumstances. In the first place, the southerners, as
a rule, dislike the northerners, despise them, feel, in fact,
antipathy towards them, to a degree till now little understood. They consider them *snobbish*, pedantic, pushing, and
vulgar—not gentlemen, in short ; and though this sentiment seems absurd enough when we look at their own pro-

ceedings, and the degraded condition both as to comfort and education of four-fifths of their own white population, yet it exists in great strength, and is traceable in part to the fact that *they* sprung from *Cavalier*, and their rivals from *Puritan*, colonisation ; in part to the change wrought in the northerners by the large infusion of Irish and German immigration, and in part to the irritating relation of debtor and creditor which prevails so largely. In fact, the southern planters feel towards the northern merchants and settlers somewhat as spendthrift nobles feel towards the thriving tradesman who lends them money ; or as landed gentry, out at elbows and fond of hunting and hospitality, feel towards the mushroom manufacturer who first becomes the mortgagee and afterwards the purchaser of their patrimonial estates.

But there was more than this. The South had a double interest in the acquisition of fresh territory in a tropical direction, and, for this purpose, in retaining the command of the federal government ; the North had no such interest — rather the contrary. It is the peculiarity of slave cultivation that it can only be profitably applied to virgin soils, which yield their produce abundantly even to the roughest tillage ; for the more careful and elaborate contrivances of husbandry neither the slave nor his master is sufficiently intelligent and energetic. This is especially true of cotton-planting. Every five or six years the plantation is moved; new land is taken into cultivation ; and as soon as the available amount within the state has been overrun and exhausted, new territory must be acquired. Besides this motive there is another, which in practice has been nearly equally influential. It is only by the acquisition of new territory, *out of which new States can be formed*, that the slaveholding section of the community could hope to maintain that equality in the Senate of which the increase of the free-population had long since deprived it in the House of Representatives. Hence, since slave products can only be cultivated in a hot climate, extension towards the South by means of conquest, annexation, filibustering, or purchase, became almost a law of existence to the slave states, and has now for nearly a generation been the leading idea of their policy. Thus the passion for conquest and territorial aggrandisement, which has prompted many of the most disreputable proceedings of the United States, is less attributable to the naturally aggressive and domineering tendency of democracy than to the political and economical exigencies of slavery. To this domestic institution we must trace the insidious settlement, then the treacherous rebellion, then the unprincipled annexation of Texas, out of which three slave states are ultimately to be formed. To this, also, was owing the Mexican war, which ended in the acquisition from that weak government of the district now called "New Mexico,"—to which we are assured that Sonora and Coahuila are soon to be added. The infraction of the "Missouri Compromise," in defiance of the most solemn engagement, and all the astounding atrocities of the border ruffians in Kansas; the "Ostend Manifesto," with the unparalleled audacity of its claim on Cuba, and its denunciation of any European intervention on the American continents; the piratical attempts of Lopez upon Cuba and of Walker upon Nicaragua; the "Central American" dispute with this country; the indecent application of the President to Congress for funds to purchase the coveted island which Spain had refused to sell ; the insolent and *ungentlemanly* appointment as ambassador to Madrid of that very M. Soulé who had made himself so conspicuous in applauding the filibustering expedition of Lopez, and probably in aiding it ; to say nothing of several minor acts of greed and *outrecuidance;*—all had their origin in the slave-holding

necessity for fresh territory, to uphold the endangered "institution," and the supremacy that was fast slipping away.

Slavery, too, must bear the largest share of blame for the
more frequent brutalities and the increasing barbarism of
American society, of which we saw some dawning specimens
under the presidency of General Jackson.   The extent to
which these have now reached, the frequency of their occurrence, the rank of life of the perpetrators, and above all the
trivial attention they excite, and the faint reprobation (if
any) which they call down, constitute in our judgment the
most revolting and ominous features in the social condition
of the great Republic.   Much allowance, no doubt, must be
made for the natural roughness of men who have made
themselves the pioneers of civilisation, who have lived much
alone, or in the woods with natures as uncultivated as their
own, and whose whole life has been a ceaseless, hand-to-
hand, mortal conflict with the forest and the jungle, with
wild Indians and wild beasts.   Fierce enmities, untamed
passions, and savage outbreaks may often be expected from
such men, even when called to govern or to legislate for
hastily formed communities.   But the atrocities of which
we speak are by no means exclusively or principally perpetrated among the settlers in the new states that have been
conquered by hard labour from the forest and the prairie.
They are seen even in the streets of New York and Washington, and are far more common in the South than in the
West, in Texas than in Illinois ; and they are *not* met with,
or very rarely, even in the remotest provinces of Canada.

No doubt, too, much must be attributed to that intolerance of opposition and impatience of control which absolute democracy usually engenders, to those habits of insolent oppression which always spring up where " the tyranny
of the majority" is without a check, and to that coarseness
of manners which cannot fail to spread where the lower,

O

and not the upper classes set the fashion and rule the state. But democracy is enthroned in as absolute power in the New England states as in the South, and yet the exhibitions of savagery which have so dishonoured America are of the rarest possible occurrence there. We find them almost exclusively either among slave-holders or in the slave states; and can trace them directly to the essential adjuncts of slavery, viz., the possession of absolute power, the fury generated by a haunting though unacknowledged fear, and the habitual association from childhood with a race systematically kept at the lowest ebb of intellect and morals. The children of the planters and southern gentlemen are brought among slaves, themselves brutal and degraded, and on whom they are able and are permitted to exercise, without remonstrance or fear of resistance, their capricious passions, whether those passions prompt to cruelty or lust. We need say no more, after these few words, than quote one sentence from Mr Olmsted's last work. " How," he asks, " can men retain the most essential quality of true manhood who daily, without remonstrance or interference, see men beaten whose position renders effective resistance totally impracticable—and not only men, but women too? Is it not partially the result of this that self-respect seldom seems to suggest to an angry man at the South that he should use any thing like magnanimity or fair play in a quarrel?" In fact, the entire natural education of the southern slave-holders seems directed to teach their hot blood to give way to the first impulse of passion; and how can we expect those who have learned this lesson upon coloured men to abstain from practising it upon white men when aroused?

Now, with the inevitable tendency of these causes in our minds, let us turn to their practical operation, and see how they have undermined the natural feelings of freedom, humanity, and justice. We wish to avoid all highly coloured pictures, and to say no more than is required to exemplify our position. Details may be found in Olmsted's works, and in the columns of *Southern* newspapers. We will merely *allude* to the habitual violation of postage secrecy, under cover of both law and practice, for the detection of any documents conveying anti-slavery opinions; to the entire suppression, by the promptest measures of Lynch law, of the faintest approach to discussion or to the expression of opinion, even in private society, on the forbidden topic ; to the tarring and feathering, the forcible banishment, the cruel scourging of peaceable citizens, and even of venerable clergymen, who were *suspected* merely (and often wrongfully) of spreading abolition doctrines or of only counselling humanity and moderation—for, alas, all these things are of daily occurrence and of unquestioned notoriety ; so that not even in Rome, in Russia, or in Austria, is personal freedom and security such a hideous mockery as in the southern states of the North American Republic. We *hear* of the burning alive of an itinerant hawker in Texas not two years ago, for the supposed crime of encouraging a fugitive; but as the story, though not doubted, has not been actually proved or avowed, we will not endorse it. But the progress from ordinary fair and decent duels with pistols—first, to savage encounters with rifles, revolvers, and bowie-knives, when the disabled combatant is butchered in cold blood on the ground, and no spectator cries shame upon the murderer,—and then to stabbing or shooting an antagonist in the street by surprise and from behind, with not even a pretence of combat or fair play,—this progress is as notorious as it is significant, and no man seems shocked or astonished at the point which has been reached. We need only remind our readers of the SICKLES tragedy two years ago, and of the sympathy and prompt acquittal accorded to the murderer, who, though applauded for butchering the paramour, lost all his popularity by forgiving the wife. In many parts of the Union, assassination, with or without notice, has become nearly as common as in Italy in former days.

Burning alive is now the *recognised* punishment for slaves who assault or slay their masters, if indeed they are not shot in the act. Not many months ago, Mr Olmsted tells us,* a Negro who had attacked his master, just as Mr Brooks attacked Mr Sumner, from behind and killed him on the spot, was roasted by a slow fire, in the presence of several thousand slaves, and many magistrates, clergymen, and other chief inhabitants. The most moderate newspapers of the district justified the deed ; others applauded it, partly on the ground that it " was no act of an excited multitude, but the cool, calm, deliberate proceeding of one thousand citizens ;" and the editor of one of these journals —*a Methodist preacher*—declared that " the punishment was unequal to the crime ;' and that he should have suggested tearing the criminal to pieces with red-hot pincers, or cutting off a limb at a time, and burning them all in a heap." It is not by ferocious actions like this, *but by the way in which they are received and spoken of by the community at large,* that we can judge of the awful state of feeling produced by the mingled lawlessness and terror which prevails in the slave-holding districts of the Union. This remark applies with especial force to the last indication of the brutal temper cultivated by slavery, to which we shall need to refer in illustration of our argument. The barbarous and cowardly outrage committed by Mr Brooks on Mr Sumner in the Senate-house at Washington is in every body's recollection ;—how, in retalliation for a speech made in the Senate, a senator was assaulted by an intruding

* Vol. iii., p. 442.

member of the House of Representatives, taken from behind
and unawares while seated at his desk, and incapable of
self-defence, caned on the head till he was insensible and
nearly dead—the assailant being accompanied by a friend,
and the rest of the senators (with one single exception)
watching the completion of the outrage without interference.   This scene, occurring in the Parliament of a great
nation, was sufficiently characteristic and disgusting; but
the scene itself was nothing to what followed.   Mr Brooks
was called upon to pay—300 dollars; he was obliged to
resign his seat in Congress, but was immediately re-elected
by a vast majority; all the southern newspapers applauded
his act as "*chivalrous*, noble, gallant, and courageous;"
public meetings were everywhere held to present fulsome
addresses of admiration to him ; and lastly, the ladies of
South Carolina (the state he represented) presented him
with a splendid gold-headed cane, in lieu of the one he *had
broken* over his victim's head, inscribed with the words,
" Hit him again !"   Mr Olmsted's remarks on this matter
are too pertinent to be omitted.   " The late Mr Brooks's
character should be honestly considered, now that personal
enmity towards him is impossible.   That he was courteous,
accomplished, warm-hearted, and hot-blooded, dear as a
friend, and fearful as an enemy, may be believed by all;
but in the South his name is never mentioned without the
term *gallant* or *courageous*, *spirited* or *noble*, being also
applied to it.   Why is this?   The truth is, we include in
these terms a habit of mind *which slavery has rendered,* in a
great degree, *obsolete in the South.*   The man who has been
accustomed from childhood to see men beaten when they
have no chance to defend themselves ; to hear men accused,
vituperated, and reproved, who dare not open their lips in
self-defence or reply; who is accustomed to see other men
whip women without interference, remonstrance, or any

expression of indignation,—must have a certain quality, which is an essential point of personal honour with us, greatly blunted, if not entirely destroyed. The same quality which we detest in the assassination of an enemy is essentially constant in all slavery. It is found in effecting one's will with another, when he cannot, if he would, defend himself. Accustomed to this every hour of their lives, southerners do not feel magnanimity and the 'fair-play' impulse to be a necessary part of the quality of 'spirit,' courage, or nobleness. By 'spirit' they apparently mean only passionate vindictiveness of character, and by 'gallantry' mere intrepidity." *Generosity to the weak,* which lies at the root of chivalry and true manliness, must become extinct in them.

Slavery is responsible in yet another way for the deterioration and repellant coarseness of American manners, especially in the South, in yet another mode, and one that deserves far more study than it has yet received. The entire white population of the Slave States now exceeds eight millions. Of these the actual slave-holders (who are under 350,000 in number) with their families do not amount to two millions—probably not to much more than 1,500,000. What is the character and condition of the remaining six millions and a half? They have no slaves, and are too poor to buy any ; they live in a land where the existence of slaves renders all agricultural labour a dis-honour, and therefore nearly an impossibility to the white man, however destitute, or however industriously inclined ; —how, then, do they subsist, and what is their social status as to comfort and reputation ! Mr Olmsted's last volume answers this question very fully. A certain number are respectable mechanics, shopkeepers, and small tradesmen in the towns ; many keep liquor-shops and taverns ; others follow any occupations that are not menial ; some are sportsmen, or keep bloodhounds for the purpose of hunting runaway Negroes ; but the great majority are squatters on such soil as they find unoccupied or can purchase. But as these are nearly always in the lowest state of social and moral degradation,—ignorant, debauched, and idle, and very mischievous to the Negroes, whom they demoralise and supply with drink,—the planters are exceedingly anxious to remove them from their estates. They buy up their small plots of land, or bribe them to disappear ; and the poor wretches are thus driven yearly farther and farther from civilisation, and live in log-huts on the produce of such grain as they can raise from their clearings and patches of soil, and such game as they can kill and exchange for rum or whisky ; and sink into a depth of squalor, wretchedness, and barbarism which teaches the very slaves to despise them, and which would appear to be almost without a parallel, except *perhaps* in Ireland, in her worst districts and her worst times. These men often emigrate to new states : they become the "Border Ruffians" of Missouri ; they swarm in the lowest haunts of New Orleans and other cities ; they help to constitute the rowdies, bullies, gamblers, and murderers of most portions of the Union ; but *wherever they go, they are voters,* and wherever they go, they lower the tone of manners, morals, decency, and comfort. Too poor to be proprietors, too proud to be domestics, too white to be industrious labourers for hire in a slave-land, too ignorant and too wretched to aspire to a better position, they form the growing gangrene of that great nation. They are the very spontaneous seed-beds and disseminators of brutality and filth ; yet they are the natural product of a system under which industry is discredited by its association with "niggerdom" and servitude.

Such having become the condition of the country to be

ruled, it remains to be seen what manner of men are now
its rulers. George Washington was a great and good man,
firm in his purposes, righteous in his means; and his
fellow-statesmen were worthy to be his colleagues. Andrew
Jackson was neither good nor great, but he was *strong;* he
was consistent and clear in his designs, and unflinching in
the promptitude and vigour with which he carried them
out. He was narrow, but not bad: he was virulent, but
not mean. James Buchanan is corrupt, unscrupulous, and
feeble; from the day of his inauguration, he has shown
neither capacity, principle, nor dignity; he has been altogether an evil and unworthy man; nothing so poor has yet
sat in the presidential chair. He was elected mainly on
the ground of the "Ostend Manifesto," and his understood
subserviency to the cause of "slavery extension," and consequent annexation at the South. He did all he could to
redeem his pledge. He connived at the filibustering
expeditions of Walker to Nicaragua in the most transparent
manner; he liberated that pirate, when arrested and
brought back; he was silent and inactive when the same
man was received with public ovations in the chief cities
of the Union. He endeavoured to persuade Congress to
·intrust him with thirty millions of dollars wherewith to
purchase Cuba from Spain (Spain having already resented
the proposal as a flagrant insult), and intimated in his
message that if not *sold*, it might perhaps be *taken*. He
got up the Central American Dispute with Great Britain
with the view of obtaining sole command over the Isthmus
and the adjoining territory. He not only encouraged and
assisted the border ruffians of Missouri in the most open
·manner in their lawless violences against Kansas;—he
actually employed the United States troops in putting down
the legitimate self-defence of their outraged victims; and
endeavoured to force through Congress a bill to legalise and

confirm the proceedings of the slave-holding rioters of Lecompton,—acting throughout the whole affair, not as the Chief Magistrate of the Republic, but as the shameless nominee of the Slave-extensionists. Happily, through the firmness of the Free-soilers, he failed, and Kansas is now a free state within the Union. It is believed—indeed, scarcely denied, and almost proved—that he owed his election mainly to corruption exercised in an unusually reckless and extravagant fashion in his native state of Pennsylvania. It is notorious that bribery of all kinds, both of constituencies and of assemblies, has become fearfully rife during his administration.* It is on record that a committee (the ' Covode ' Committee, as it was called) was appointed in 1859, by the House of Representatives, to inquire into alleged malversation of funds voted for the navy, some of which were believed to have been employed in passing through the House a bill in which the President

---

* From an official report by a committee of the Legislative Assembly of the State of Wisconsin, it appears that a certain railway company obtained their charter and donation of public lands by bribing the entire Government. *Thirteen* members of the Senate received £35,000 among them in railway bonds. *Sixty* members of the Lower House received from £1000 to £2000 each. The Governor of the State received £10,000 ; his Private Secretary, £1000 ; the Lieutenant-Governor, £2000 ; the Bank Controller, £2000 ; the clerks of the House, £1000 to £2000 each. Besides this, £50,000 was distributed among "outsiders," lobby-agents, &c. The passing of the requisite bills for many railway grants through *Congress* itself, too, is openly asserted to have been managed by wholesale bribery.

Among other painful proofs of the general lowering of the standard of national integrity must not be forgotten '' Repudiation," which came into vogue between the eras of Jackson and Buchanan. The defaulting states were ten in number : of these Pennsylvania, Illinois, Louisiana, Maryland, and Alabama, resumed their payments to the public creditor after a time ; but Indiana compromised for about half the amount of her debt ; and Michigan, Arkansas, Florida, and Mississippi repudiated their obligations altogether, and are still fraudulent debtors, though now very wealthy.

was interested ; and more to have been abused by unfair
contracts to favoured electioneers ; and though much was
not proved, and though Mr Buchanan vehemently protested
against the investigation into such charges, yet enough
came out before that committee, and was embodied in their
report, to connect him most discreditably with some very
ill-favoured transactions.   Among other documents was a
private letter from a friendly politician to the President,
advising that a certain contract should be given to a certain
firm in Philadelphia, as it would be worth 450 votes to the
administration in the coming election.   This letter was
endorsed by the President, and forwarded by him to the
Secretary of the Navy.   We cannot go into details ; but
the revelation of systematic jobbing at the dockyards, with
the full knowledge of the chiefs, was something startling.
And, as if to place the general conclusions beyond doubt,
Mr Buchanan wrote his curious ' Pittsburg ' letter, deplor-
ing in the strongest language the spread of corruption and
the general decline of integrity among public men.   Finally,
the recent deliberate treason of three members of the
cabinet, and the proved frauds of one of them, need only to
be recalled to mind to give us a conception how deeply
immorality of every sort must have eaten into the heart of
political circles in America.

NEARLY half a generation has elapsed since the above pages
were published, and it can scarcely be said that any of the
political evils and dangers therein signalised have diminished.
On the contrary, in spite of the energetic efforts of good
citizens, the progress of corruption in the Legislatures, the
Judicial Board, Municipal Government, and Commercial
life, would seem to have been rapid and appalling.   The

following summary of facts and authorities will suffice to bear out the statement ;*—and it does not include some of the worst and latest disclosures, for which we must refer to the pages of the *North American Review* for the last four years.

" America is, *par excellence*, the land of amateur administration. Everything there — public undertakings, local rule, central government, distribution of justice and law, to a great extent even war itself—is managed by vestries, committees, associations, by untrained and improvised volunteers, in short. In the United States, as we all know, any man may become anything ; and most men in the course of their lives are many things. Judges, generals, sheriffs, municipal *employés* of all kinds, presidents, surveyors of taxes, revenue officers, are selected and created *pro re natâ*, with an utter disregard of preparatory instruction or professional requirements. No qualification appears to be needed, and no antecedents appear to be considered a disqualification. We in Great Britain go far enough in this direction ; but our Civil Service, at least, is in a great degree an exception. Its members are permanent, belong to a sort of hierarchy, are trained by long practice to their work, have a decided, and on the whole a very salutary, *esprit de corps*, and now by degrees are becoming picked men. In America, every civil servant of the State holds office at the precarious hazard of party victory; he gets and gives up his appointment at every change of Government ; he can count at most upon only a very few years of official life. The entire administrative staff thus consists, and in the main must consist, of ' 'prentice hands.'† Few can

* " Political Problems," pp. 275-288.

† The following extracts give the American view of the facts of the case in far stronger language than I should have presumed to use :—
" The revenue department of this Government has been most

remain in place long enough either to learn their work or to love their work, or to have any professional pride in doing it well and honourably.

America is a crucial example of self-government — or government by amateurs. New York is a crucial specimen even in America. Two or three years ago we were presented in the pages of the *North American Review* with a startling picture of the municipal government of that city, drawn by the hand of a countryman who had studied it for the sake of describing it, and, if possible, of rescuing his

---

shamefully maltreated, and by all political parties, as they have successively come into power. Its various institutions, instead of subserving the public interests, as they should, have been converted into hospitals, alms-houses, political fortresses, and places of refuge (if not refuse). Instead of capable officers, honest, respectable, and faithful — brawling politicians, broken-down hacks, and imbecile persons, have filled the places, through favouritism, nepotism, or corruption of some kind. The Government has lavished its funds, and for the purpose of having its business faithfully transacted, it has appropriated an ample amount for that object; but intrigue and favouritism have almost neutralised its legitimate and intended effects in several ways. Incompetent and inefficient men are foisted in ; they constitute the corps of loafers, whose time hangs idle on their hands, and who are continually hovering about the industrious, and are serious obstacles to these. By means of personal influence, and plenty of time to wield it, they generally secure the fullest salaries, especially at a season when salaries are raised. Dishonest persons are another corps, embezzlers, peculators, corrupt or venal ; these insinuate themselves into all branches as furtively as Ulysses managed to elude the searching hands of Polyphemus. Intemperate people also use the public fund, not for their families, but to distress and tantalise them. Partisans, steeped in the elixir of ignorance, disgrace the public books with their scrawling chirography, their blundering arithmetic, their dislocated orthography, and their downright assassination of grammar. The services of such seem to be venerated, and, therefore, they are very apt to sit in the highest places, and to be most richly remunerated for their actual impositions upon their great almoner, their direct employer. Nor is this all ; they are generally the most strongly fortified in

State from the deep disgrace and danger of such unexampled incapacity and corruption. Every man there seems to be an elector. There are in the city 77,000 foreign-born voters and 52,000 native ones. The 'grog-shop' interest alone can send to the poll 25,000 votes. The great bulk of the city property is in the hands of about 15,000 men, who are thus at the mercy of the 129,000 ; who for the most part have no property and pay no taxes. Seven electioneerers or wire-pullers, it is affirmed, manage all elections, all appointments, and, directly or indirectly, all

---

their positions, while the well-qualified, quiet, faithful, unobtrusive incumbent is often the first to be removed—for what? To make room for a green hand, of course inexperienced, and perhaps unable to make good the vacancy at any time or by any discipline of training. This makes the official business limp, and perhaps inflicts serious damage upon it. Nor has the industrious, competent, faithful victim been removed from an easy and lucrative, but from a decidedly laborious and meagrely-paid station ; and if it be too difficult for his inexperienced successor, the business will be diminished, or he will be provided with an assistant, or another will be appointed his substitute, while he is transferred to an easier, and very likely more lucrative post.

"Suffice it to say, that the Government appropriates enough money to pay for the *aggregate* services rendered to it, but the appropriation is so unequally and unjustly distributed that they who do the most work, and the best qualified, get scanty salaries, while the sinecure, semi-sinecure, and ill-qualified drones realise large and altogether disproportionate compensation. It is so—truly so, incontrovertibly so, lamentably so. Very few do the work, and are poorly paid ; they work in and out of hours closely and incessantly ; salaries small. Others have most of the day for yawning, gadding, spinning yarns to the annoyance of others, snapping beans or corn, and reading newspapers, or writing for them, to while away the official interval. Soon as the hour of three arrives they are off quick as a flock of ducks at the discharge of a gun. They reap largely at the month's end, while the workers who have been employed during their neighbour's *ennui*, or who have been left behind, still plod on their drudgery, and at the end of the month receive but an unjust, a miserable pittance. Talk about injustice to factory

jobs. The members of the Town Council are for the most part young, vulgar, uneducated men, loafers or tradesmen of the inferior sort, ready to do any dirty work, and highly paid for the work they do.

" There is a certain air (says the native authority from which we draw our facts) about most of these young Councilmen which, in the eyes of a New-Yorker, stamps them as belonging to what has been styled of late years ' our ruling class '—butcher-boys who have got into politics, bar-keepers who have taken a leading part in primary ward-meetings, young fellows who hang about engine-houses and billiard-rooms."

---

operatives ; the custom-house clerk who does the work of others that really receive the pay, is as unjustly treated as the operative. There are two iniquities: the work is unequally distributed, and the pay is unequally distributed.

" From President Jackson's time to the present, nearly forty years, the partisan obligations of the candidate for office have been held to be of more consequence than his qualifications for the place for which he is a candidate, and every administrative department of the Government has been 'used as an instrument of political or party patronage,' the discontinuance of which system was one of the objects in view in the appointment of this committee. The evil effects of this custom of discharging well-trained officers, and of appointing unskilled persons in their places, has been well described by the present head of the Treasury Department.

" Secretary M'Culloch says—' The importance of *retaining tried and experienced clerks* can hardly be overrated, and the estimation in which such are held by business men is too often exemplified by their withdrawal from the department under the inducement of salaries offered them much greater than existing laws permit them to receive from the Government. There have been 531 resignations since January 1866, many of them by persons competent and of considerable experience in their respective duties. Could ample salaries be paid and permanence of employment assured, independent of political questions, there could be no difficulty in organising the department on a basis greatly superior in point of efficiency than any private establishment. *A single experienced clerk can often perform with ease duties that could be but indifferently discharged by several inexperienced persons.*' "—*Report of Select Committee of Congress.*

The government of the city appears to be in a condition of chaotic coufusion.

" The Board of Aldermen, seventeen in number, the Board of twenty-four Councilmen, the twelve Supervisors, the twenty-one members of the Board of Education, are so many independent legislative bodies, elected by the people. The police are governed by four Commissioners, appointed by the Governor for eight years. The charitable and reformatory institutions of the city are in charge of four Commissioners, whom the City Comptroller appoints for five years. The Commissioners of the central park, eight in number, are appointed by the Governor for five years. Four Commissioners, appointed by the Governor for eight years, manage the Fire Department. There are also five Commissioners of Pilots, two appointed by the Board of Underwriters and three by the Chamber of Commerce. The finances of the city are in charge of the Comptroller, whom the *people* elect for four years. The street department has at its head one Commissioner, who is appointed by the Mayor for four years. Three Commissioners, appointed by the Mayor, manage the Croton Aqueduct department. The law-officer of the city, called the Corporation Counsel, is elected by the *people* for three years! Six Commissioners, appointed by the Governor for six years, attend to the immigration from foreign countries. To these has been recently added a Board of Health, the members of which are appointed by the Governor. Was there ever such a hodgepodge of a government before in the world? "—*North American Review*, Oct. 1866.

It will surprise no one, then, to learn that, under such a system, things are ill-done, done extravagantly, paid for, but not done at all, and that corruption and jobbery (of which detailed and well-authenticated specimens are given) have reached a pitch of shamelessness, lavishness, and method, never, we believe, yet recorded of any other land. The net result is, that in thirty-six years the taxation of the county and city of New York (identical areas) has increased from 2½ dollars per inhabitant to 40 dollars. In 1830 the municipal government cost half-a-million of dollars, in 1865 it cost more than forty millions. Yet in spite of this enormous expenditure, in spite of a permanent *democratic* majority of 30,000, which might be expected to look after the interests of the masses, many of the public institutions, and much of the poorer portion of the city, are in a condition at once perilous and disgraceful.

The same respectable authority which we have already quoted returns to the charge in a subsequent number, and writes thus :—

" The disgraceful character of the municipal government of New York is notorious. The absolute exclusion of all honest men from any practical coutrol of affairs in that city, and the supremacy in the Common Council of pick-pockets, prize-fighters, emigrants, runners, pimps, and the lowest class of liquor-dealers, are facts which admit of no question. But many respectable citizens of New York have been accustomed to console themselves with the belief that at least one department of the local government remained incorrupt ; that the judiciary could still be depended upon ; and that, whatever might be the fate of the public at the hands of aldermen, justice was yet impartially administered between man and man."—*North American Review,* July 1867.

The writer goes on to show, by a quantity of disreputable histories, traced through many years, how far this comfortable supposition is wide of the truth. There are several distinct courts in New York having separate jurisdictions ; and in all the judges are elected. They have considerable irregular patronage, and several among them abuse it shamefully ; the incompetence of some of them is notorious, and the partiality of others equally so ; they are almost invariably and manifestly very inferior both in capacity and knowledge of law, to the barristers who plead before them ; and it is a recognised fact that to succeed in your cause before particular judges you must employ particular counsel. Direct bribery—to judges as well as to judicial officers—has been not unknown in some cases, and is believed in many more: and though, no doubt, the majority of judges are trustworthy, and the majority of decisions pure and equitable, still the occurrence, and the easy possibility, of the abuses mentioned, must taint the whole administration of justice.

" To come down to the present time (continues our authority), it is indisputable that most of the judges in charge of criminal business in New York are coarse, uneducated men, knowing nothing of law except what they have picked up in their experience on the bench. One of the best of them was a butcher till he became a police-justice; another was formerly a bar-keeper. As a rule, they are excessively conceited and overbearing, and in some cases positively brutal in their demeanour. The officers in attendance naturally take their tone from their superiors, and treat every one who enters the court-room with a roughness which makes attendance on such places ineffably disgusting."

The Annual Report of the Police Commissioners for 1865, an official document, and therefore naturally guarded and moderate in its language, sums up its account of matters in New York thus :—

" In no other city does the machinery of criminal justice so signally fail to restrain or punish serious and capital offences. . . . Property is fearfully menaced by fire and robberies, and persons are in startling peril from criminal violence. This lamentable state of things is due, in a great measure, to a tardy and inefficient administration of justice. . . . As our laws and institutions are administered, they do not afford adequate protection to persons or property. Some remedy must be found and applied, or life in the metropolis will drift rapidly towards the condition of barbarism."

We have heard lately that some of the better and bolder class of citizens, roused to action by the increasing impunity with which crimes and outrages of the worst description are committed, have adopted the usual American remedy in

such extreme cases, and have organised themselves into a
"Vigilance Committee" to enforce the execution of the
law, and, if need be, to take it into their own hands.
Some relief, it is said, has already been obtained from the
dread of this new *imperium in imperio ;* but the state of
affairs is bad enough still, if the following picture, from a
source usually disposed to look with favour and sympathy,
rather than with severity, on American institutions and
character in general, can be trusted :—

"The state of affairs in this city (New York) is such that nothing any one man can do will effect much improvement, and the
poison is extending through the State. The present sheriff,
O'Brien by name, has served six months in the penitentiary, and
was a notorious rowdy, and is the personal friend of a very large
proportion of the roughs who find their way into gaol. His de-
puties, who are all Irishmen, are mostly pugilists, or ruffians of
the lowest type. One of his old friends, a man named Real, and
a member of a notorious gang of criminals known as the ' Nine-
teenth-street Gang,' is now in gaol under sentence of death for
the cowardly murder of a policeman in cold blood, and the day
was fixed for his execution, and all the arrangements made, when
proceedings were stayed under a writ of error; but the sheriff's
personal relations with the prisoner were such that he could not
be present at the execution, and had committed the superintend-
ence of it to other hands. There is hardly an office of any value
in the city government now which is not held by Irishmen of a
very low class, and I believe it is the opinion of leading democratic
politicians here of American birth that no more native Americans
can be elected hereafter. The three leading managers, however,
who distribute the nominations, are natives, but men of the worst
character. Strangely enough, in the one remaining court in which
people have confidence, and in which the judges are men of high
character and of learning—the Common Pleas—the three judges
are Irishmen. It is probably owing to this fact that the court
has escaped defilement so long ; but I have heard within a day or
two, on good authority, that it has been determined that no
further indulgence shall be extended to it, and that the youngest
of the three shall be turned out to make room for a young scamp

recently admitted to the bar, and the son of one of the most notoricus plunderers of the municipal treasury. As I have frequently told you, more than one judge of the Supreme Court is purchasable by the highest bidder, and one of them has now grown so bold in his sale of himself, and is making such an open trade of his decisions, that capital is at last getting alarmed. Several of the great railroad companies are transferring their offices to Boston, so as to get their assets and stock out of his reach or that of his satellites. In fact, the state of things has grown so bad that many leading men talk of quitting the bar."— *Daily News' Correspondent*, May 4, 1869.

Of railroad management in America we need not speak in any detail. It is far worse than ours—not immaculate—has ever been. It appears to present nearly the same features— waste, swindling, " financing," " stock-watering," ruinous Parliamentary conflicts—on a still more gigantic scale ; adding another which we as yet have not, namely, Parliamentary corruption. It is no secret that bribery to a startling extent, and shameless in form, is habitually practised by the several " rings," as they are called, or banded cliques, on the members of the State Legislatures. Mr Charles Adams, in a paper now lying before us, affirms that last year a bribe of this sort, to the value of 150,000 dollars, was paid to a single member of the New York Assembly.* There are in America 37,000 miles of rail-

---

* In 1868, the Senate of New York appointed a committee to investigate the charges then openly circulated of the bribery of senators by railroad promoters and companies. The committee reported that "large sums of money were expended for corrupt purposes by parties interested in railway legislation ; that lobbyists were thus enriched, and in some cases received money on the false pretence that the votes of the senators were to be thereby influenced ; but that there was no proof of the actual bribery of any *senators.*" They go on, however, to point out that, as the law stands, it is next to impossible to prove bribery; and conclude, "that some legislation is necessary to prevent the deposit of large sums of money with members of the lobby *for the purpose of corruption.*"

ways, which have cost about £300,000,000 sterling. Their working expenses usually reach seventy per cent. of their gross receipts :—in England the proportion is generally under fifty per cent. Notwithstanding this, they appear to pay far better dividends—habitually, it is said, more than ten per cent. on their *bona fide* capital. Accidents are, however, far more frequent there than here, in spite of a much lower average of speed ; twenty-one passengers yearly being killed in New York and Massachusetts (for instance) against five in Great Britain. We will content ourselves with a single quotation from an elaborate (American) account of " railroad inflation " in that country.

" The operations in the Erie line have long since degenerated into barefaced, gigantic swindling.* . . . . The Credit Mobilier is understood to be building the Pacific Railroad. . . . . but who constitute this Credit Mobilier ? It is but another name for the Pacific Railroad ' ring.' The members of it are in Congress ; they are trustees for the bondholders, they are directors, they are stockholders, they are contractors ; in Washington they vote the subsidies ; in New York they receive them ; upon the Plains they expend them ; in the Credit Mobilier they divide them. . Ever-shifting characters, they are ever ubiquitous—now engineering a bill, and now a bridge—they receive money into one hand as a corporation, and pay it into the other as a contractor. Humanly speaking, the whole thing seems to be a species of thimble-rig, with this difference from the ordinary arrangement, that whereas commonly the ' little joker' is never found under the thimble which may be turned up, in this case he is sure to be found, turn up which thimble we may. Under one name or another a ring of some seventy persons is struck, at whatever point the Union Pacific is approached. As stockholders they own the road, as mortgagees they have a lien upon it, as directors they contract for its construction, and as members of the Credit Mobilier they build it. . . . . Here is every vicious element of railroad construction and management—costly construction, entailing future taxation

---

* A really frightful picture of the frauds perpetrated by the Erie Railway directors appeared in *Fraser's Magazine* for May 1869.

on trade; tens of millions of fictitious capital; a road built on
the sale of its bonds, and with the aid of subsidies: here is every
element of cost recklessly exaggerated, and the whole at some
future day is to make itself felt as a burden on the trade which it
is to create; and will surely hereafter constitute a source of corruption in the politics of the land, and a resistless power in its
legislature. . . . Figures, in the skilful hands of railroad officials,
seem made, like language in the mouth of a diplomatist, not to
express truth, but to conceal it. One who has puzzled over them
long and patiently writes, in language not too strong :—'The
reports of the companies are not always to be had, and even when
attainable, are so ingeniously devised to deceive, that only severe
labour enables one to discover where the legerdemain is accomplished. The system is bad enough, but its administration is a
perfect pest-house of corruption; the dishonesty is almost
incredible, and is practised without need or profit, frequently from
mere habit.' "—*North American Review*, January 1869.

The evils arising from the system on which the Civil
Service of the Federal Government is conducted are so
notorious, are so strongly felt, that a great effort was made
a few years ago to pass Mr Jenckes' Bill, with the double
object of securing capacity by competitive examination for
all nominees, and honesty and zeal by some more permanent
tenure of office. At present, as is well known—we rely
merely on American authorities—the Government officials,
almost from the highest to the lowest, change with each
change of president or party in power. They are by
universal consent ill-paid, and usually ill-qualified, with
little or no independence, little motive for exertion, little
opportunity for distinction, but unfortunately much
opportunity for illicit gain. They are very numerous, but
usually very inefficient. It is openly stated, and not
denied, that of the vast sums collected both by the Customs
and Inland Revenue officers, a considerable proportion
never reaches the coffers of the State.* The *New York*

---

* According to Mr Well's Report, the average cost of collecting
the revenue is not extravagant, however. It amounted in 1868 to

Imperialist avers that—

" Not one of all the despotisms of the Old World employs such a locust swarm of officials, and not one has its various business so infamously ill-done."

And again—

" In France, under the Imperial Government, the full amount of every tax is collected and paid into the Treasury. In America, under a Democratic Government, the Treasury loses fifty millions every year of the tax justly due on the single article of whisky, and fifty millions more in other departments of the revenue service; to say nothing of the uncounted sums abstracted from the State, Municipal, and County taxes throughout the country."

The *Springfield Republican* says that—

" Lincoln's Secretary of the Interior used to declare that, if he dared, he could run his department with half its force of clerks, and for half its cost. M'Culloch might have put it even stronger as regards his office. General Walker (in another branch) wished to reduce twelve clerks, but Congress men came rushing to the rescue, and prevented the retrenchment."

The *San Francisco Times*, in the course of a long and bold denunciation of the general corruption, says :—

· " It has come at last almost to this, that the mass of the public expect venality from public officials, and are agreeably dissappointed when they find an honest man. The accursed system of rotation in office has sapped the honesty of the people, and thousands have descended so far in the scale of morality that

---

nearly 5 per cent. on the nett receipts for the internal revenue, and rather more than 4½ for the customs. This is lower than the cost in France, and somewhat higher than that in England. " It has been demonstrated again and again," says an American writer, " that our tax and tariff laws call for 400,000,000 dollars of revenue annually, and that but 300,000,000 dollars reach the Treasury. That this missing hundred million dollars is lost by the incompetency and rascality of some branches of the Civil Service has also been proved."—*Hunt's Merchants' Magazine*, May 1869. New York.

they are prepared to wink at the sins of officials, because they look forward to the time when they themselves will feed and fatten at the public crib."

It is in no spirit of ungenerous Pharisaism that I have referred to the errors and defects in the administrative economy of a nation, so many of whose characteristics are but reflections and exaggerations of our own ; but because ideas and principles can often be best judged when studied in their most extreme manifestations.

It is, however, important to consider how much of this unquestionable deterioration in the political life and political institutions of America is traceable not to a degeneracy of the original race, but to a positive change in its elements. The Americans of the days of General Grant can scarcely be said to be the descendants of the Americans of Washington's epoch. The original Republicans who founded that great empire have been superseded rather than succeeded. We are now in a position to measure and estimate the magnitude of the transmutation.

The colonists who defied Great Britain in 1776 and established their independence in 1783 were the lineal and unspoiled descendants of the two best classes which England ever sent forth. They sprang, not only without degeneracy, but with the invigoration of a transplanted life, from the *élite* of Englishmen—the Puritans and Pilgrim Fathers who settled in New England, and the gallant and adventurous Cavaliers who colonised Virginia, Carolina, and Baltimore. Who, according to the last census just published, constitute the actual citizens of the United States in 1870 ? How many of them are the children or grandchildren, or in any way really the pure genuine descendants, of the chivalrous, religious, and high-minded Anglo-Saxons, or rather Britons, who won their independence under Washington ? We cannot say with accuracy, but almost certainly not *one-half*.

The facts are these, and they are very instructive. Taking round numbers, the entire population of the Union is 38,500,000, of which the coloured races (negro, or with more or less of negro blood, including the few Indians and Chinese) constitute as nearly as may be five millions. This element we will, for obvious reasons, leave out of consideration for the present. But what are the constituent elements of the white residue, who reach 33,500,000 ? Just one-half of them are foreigners, or born in America of foreign parents. The figures are these, as nearly as can be ascertained :—

Foreign born, ...	5,600,000
Both parents foreign, . .	9,740,000
One parent foreign, . . .	1,160,000
	16,500,000

That is, we may say, 16½ out of 33½ millions are of foreign birth or foreign parentage.

Next, we have to consider of *what* foreign origin. And if we assume, as we probably may, that the foreigners who marry Americans bear the same proportion to countries as the foreign immigrants, the result is as follows:—

	Foreign born.	Of Foreign Parents.	Total.
Ireland, ...	1,900,000	3,800,000	5,700,000
Germany, ...	1,700,000	3,400,000	5,100,000
Great Britain and Canada,	1,200,000	2,400,000	3,600,000
Rest of Europe, . . .	500,000	1,000,000	1,500,000
Miscellaneous, ...	200,000	400,000	600,000
	5,500,000	11,000,000	16,500,000

It is evident, however, that this table does not quite completely or correctly represent the extent or apportionment of the foreign element in the population. It does not take into account the grandchildren of foreign-born parents, who must be very numerous, nor the numbers of French and Spanish extraction who were incorporated by the purchase of Louisiana and the cession of Florida, nor the number of Irish (very large certainly) included among the emigrants from Canada. When we have made the requisite allowances under these heads, the proportions of blood and original nationality—the several foreign elements which now go to make up the aggregate of the citizens of the United States—will stand approximately thus:—

Original British stock, . .	46 per cent.
Of Irish extraction, . .	16 „
Of German extraction, . .	13 „
Of African extraction, . .	12 „
Of recent British extraction, .	8 „
Of French, Spanish, and others,	5 „
	100

But, as of late years, the new arrivals, especially the Irish and Germans, have proved far more prolific than the older population of the New England States, it may fairly be doubted whether more than half the present inhabitants of the United States are of real English blood. Such a change as this since the days of Washington could not possibly have taken place without entailing a change of character of almost equal magnitude, even if other circumstances had not exercised great influence also.

TURNBULL AND SPEARS, PRINTERS, EDINBURGH.

WORKS BY W. R. GREG.

ENIGMAS OF LIFE. Eighth Edition. With a Postscript. Crown 8vo. Cloth, 10s. 6d.

CONTENTS.

I. Realisable Ideals.
II. Malthus Notwithstanding.
III. Non-Survival of the Fittest.
IV. Limits and Directions of Human Development.

V. The Significance of Life.
VI. De Profundis.
VII. Elsewhere.
　 Appendix.
　 Postscript.

" What is to be the future of the human race? What are the great obstacles in the way of progress? What are the best means of surmounting these obstacles? Such, in a rough statement, are some of the problems which are more or less present to Mr Greg's mind; and although he does not pretend to discuss them fully, he makes a great many observations about them, always expressed in a graceful style, frequently eloquent, and occasionally putting old subjects in a new light, and recording the results of a large amount of reading and enquiry."—*Saturday Review*

" The whole set of Essays is at once the profoundest and the kindliest that has for some time tried to set people a thinking about themselves and their destiny."—*Daily Telegraph.*

" The essays of which we have already spoken contain perhaps more deep and new thought upon subjects of the profoundest interest than we have ever seen compressed into the like space, expressed with that perfect clearness which is the peculiar charm of the author's style, and renders him intelligible to all."—*Standard.*

POLITICAL PROBLEMS FOR OUR AGE AND COUNTRY.

In one Volume, demy 8vo, pp. 342. Cloth 10s. 6d.

CONTENTS.

I. Constitutional and Autocratic Statesmanship.
II. England's Future Attitude and Mission.
III. Disposal of the Criminal Classes.
IV. Recent Change in the Character of English Crime.
V. The Intrinsic Vice of Trade Unions.
VI. Industrial and Co-operative Partnerships.

VII. The Economic Problem.
VIII. Political Consistency.
IX. The Parliamentary Career.
X. The Price we pay for Self-government.
XI. Vestryism.
XII. Direct *versus* Indirect Taxation.
XIII. The New Régime, and how to meet it.

" A large section of the educated classes may welcome in Mr Greg a confident guide to lead them towards doctrines which they are inclined and yet afraid to accept "—*Saturday Review.*

" It is always a pleasure to read Mr Greg's political or literary writings. . . . But if you like the companionship of a robust intellect, that braces all whom it comes in contact with, and can be chivalrous enough to admire feats of strength and moral courage, whatever their object be, and if you like to commune with a political writer who is no mere political attorney, you will bear with Mr Greg's rough points, and will frankly own him to be one of the ablest of living political writers. His intellectual gifts are numerous."—*Scotsman.*

" We are always compelled to admire, but very seldom allowed to agree with Mr Greg's political writings. He is an idealogue, with the style of a consummate journalist, and the knowledge of a practised statistician."—*Spectator.*

" It is very refreshing to meet with a writer like Mr Greg, who handles the most pressing social and political questions at once acutely and profoundly, and yet with a rare amount of independence of all the sections of current opinion."—*Westminster Review, April* 1870.

" Mr Greg thinks clearly, and expresses his thoughts in vigorous language. He rarely writes on a subject without having taken considerable trouble to master its details. And the questions which, in his ' Political Problems,' he offers for solution, or attempts to solve, are of great and immediate importance. For all these reasons his book will repay study."—*North British Review, April* 1870.

THE CREED OF CHRISTENDOM : its Foundations contrasted with its Superstructure. Third Edition. With a new Introduction. In two Volumes, crown 8vo, pp. cxxiv.-156 and vi.-284. Cloth, 15s.

"We do not hesitate to say that for a man of sound mind to read this book through slowly, and to retain his belief in the verbal inspiration of the Mosaic Record, is a moral impossibility."—*Spectator.*

"His work remains a monument of his industry, his high literary power his clear intellect and his resolute desire to arrive at the truth. In its present shape, with the new Introduction, it will be still more widely read and more warmly welcomed by those who believe that in a contest between truth and error truth never can be worsted."—*Scotsman.*

LITERARY AND SOCIAL JUDGMENTS. Second (Library) Edition, in one Volume, 8vo, pp. 416, handsomely bound in cloth, price 12s. ; also a People's Edition, in small crown 8vo, cloth, 5s.

CONTENTS.

I. Madame de Stael.
II. British and Foreign Characteristics.
III. False Morality of Lady Novelists.
IV. Kingsley and Carlisle.
V. French Fiction : The Lowest Deep.
VI. Chateaubriand.

VII. M. De Tocqueville.
VIII. Why are Women Redundant ?
IX. Truth *versus* Edification.
X. The Doom of the Negro Race.
XI. Time.
XII. Good People.

"The charm of Mr Greg's writing, more especially upon political subjects, consists in no slight degree in the difficulty his readers feel in differing with him. Grant his postulates and it is nearly impossible not to grant his conclusions. His argument is 'linked reason long drawn out,' stated in language as pellucid as it is possible for language to be, interrupted by few digressions, and spoiled by no needless qualifications."—*Spectator.*

"In the essay entitled 'Doom of the Negro Race,' even those who might be most inclined to criticise his conclusions will agree that Mr Greg comes out as a publicist of very high quality indeed ; the careful preparation of facts, their lucid and orderly arrangement, and the wisdom of the political philosophy, compose a most masterly piece."—*Saturday Review.*

"Selection and discrimination become then all the more valuable from their rarity, and independently of the intrinsic interest of the articles, a volume like Mr Greg's ought to be welcomed as a protest against slipshod habits of thought and vindication of the dignity of criticism. The articles he reproduces deal rather with important and suggestive than unfamiliar subjects. In every page we can see that his works have been labours of love, and he only comes to his conclusions after carefully collecting and weighing all accessible evidence."—*Times.*

"At a time when so much intellectual power is monopolized by criticism, it is much to stand in the second rank of critics, and Mr Greg stands perhaps in the first ; for 'The Literary and Social Judgments' which he has collected from the pages of reviews and magazines, and has here republished in a permanent form, disclose the possession of many of those gifts which, possessed in full measure, refine the finely appreciative and discriminating critic, and enrich us with such criticisms as Goethe, Lessing, or Hazlitt has given. Acuteness, power of analysis, combined with sufficient synthetic power to cast the analytical results into artistic form, skill to draw fine distinctions, to express them broadly, to magnify them so as to be distinguishable by the naked eye, and to body them forth in luminous and tangible imagery—these arms make up the greater part of a critic's intellectual outfit, and these Mr Greg possesses in considerable degree."—*Scotsman.*

TRUTH versus EDIFICATION. In one Vol., fcp. 8vo, pp. 32. Cloth, 1s.

WHY ARE WOMEN REDUNDANT ? In one Vol., fcp. 8vo, pp. 40. Cloth. 1s.

TRÜBNER & CO., 57 AND 59 LUDGATE HILL, LONDON.